# Dead Men Don't Have Sex

## A Guy's Guide to Surviving Prostate Cancer

*Robert Hill*

ISBN: 1451577877
ISBN-9781451577877

*Grow old along with me!*
*The best is yet to be.*
*The last of life, for which the first was made.*

Robert Browning

This book is dedicated to Charlotte. Thank you for saving ~~my~~ our life.

# TABLE OF CONTENTS

# PROLOGUE

It rained the day I got cancer.

It was a cold, wet, miserable November morning, and the drive back from the doctor's office took forever. As my SUV inched its way through the congested city streets, I felt like I was on my hands and knees crawling toward a future I didn't understand and didn't want. The weather fit my frame of mind: cloudy with a chance of showers—man and nature in perfect harmony.

Moments earlier, three staccato words delivered in a sterile exam room had ricocheted off my eardrums and changed my life forever.

*"You've got cancer."*

I couldn't dispute it and didn't understand it. What I *didn't* know about prostate cancer would have filled a warehouse. Hell, I wasn't even sure where my prostate *was*. Questions bounced around in my mind like the rata-tat-tat of unanswered automatic weapons fire.

*Cancer?* Why would my prostate want to kill me? What did this mean for the rest of my life? And how much *"rest"* did I have? Those questions and a million more charged at me and demanded answers. I needed to regain command of the body that had decided to desert me.

I needed help. I needed it *now*.

———

# PROLOGUE

If you've picked up this book because you or someone you love has just been diagnosed with prostate cancer, relax. This book answers the questions you now have, but more importantly, it provides a road map to recovery. It picks up where your physician left off, giving you a step-by-step guide to get you from prostate cancer diagnosis, through surgery, and into recuperation. I wish someone had given *me* this book on that cold, gray November day.

Here's what you should know about me. I am not a doctor. This is not a medical book. This is a guide based solely on my experience with prostate cancer. So, why should you continue reading? Because this book answers the single most important question you have right now: *"What's it really like?"* Pull up a comfortable chair and I'll tell you all about it.

Think of this book as you would a conversation with a good friend. Someone who will tell you the good as well as the bad—*everything* you need to know to navigate this illness. But before you go any further, there's something else you should know. I am the Ike and Tina Turner of prostate cancer—*I never do anything nice and easy.* I wrote this book the hard way—through trial and sometimes comical error—as I weaved my way down the rabbit hole that is prostate cancer. My hope is that my experience makes your journey easier.

What qualifies me to write this book?

Two words: prostatic adenocarcinoma.

I was diagnosed and my cancer was classified as stage T1c with a Gleason's grade of $3+3$ = a score of 6/10. At that time, I was a forty-seven-year-old male with a 2.7 PSA (prostate-specific antigen). I had a robotic-assisted laparoscopic radical prostatectomy at USMD Hospital in Arlington, Texas.

Today, I am proud to be a cancer survivor.

———

# ACKNOWLEDGEMENTS

I wouldn't be here without the help of some amazing and talented people. First on my list is my loving wife, Charlotte. She has been by my side and done a lot of the heavy lifting. Perhaps her greatest contribution is that she helped me embrace the "new normal" that is my life today. Charlotte is my true north. A generous and giving woman who kept me pointed in the right direction and helped me find my way back home.

Next, is my son, Cole. He earned his graduate degree in growing up while I was stumbling through diagnosis, surgery, and recovery. It would have been easy for him to retreat into a well-deserved teenaged funk at this time, and no one would have thought less of him. Instead, he persevered while making good grades and maintaining a good attitude. I like to think we both matured a little as this experience tested us. And it's a curious thing to say, but I am confident that in many ways, battling cancer made us a little stronger.

Doctors Gary Price, David Lee, and Justin Lee come next. Dr. Price is the gifted Urology Associates of North Texas (UANT) urologist who *"caught the cancer early."* Dr. David Lee, formerly of UANT, now chief of urology, Penn Presbyterian Medical Center (University of Pennsylvania Health System), saved my life with the help of the da Vinci robot. Besides being an excellent surgeon, Dr. Lee exuded confidence and compassion, and humored me during the most difficult period of my life. I am proud to call him my doctor. I am prouder still to call him my friend. UANT's Dr. Justin Lee continues to this day as my partner on this cancer journey. I am Tonto to his Lone Ranger. He's a talented surgeon and gifted physician who monitors my PSA test scores and continued progress. I tell him repeatedly,

# ACKNOWLEDGEMENTS

"The prostate exam is the only test where zero is a passing grade!" I'm sure he gets tired of hearing that comment, but I never tire of saying it.

Finally, I'd like to thank my friends. Dr. Norman Vincent Peale once told a colleague facing a life-threatening illness that he needed two things. *"Get yourself a good doctor,"* Dr. Peale said. *"And get yourself a good God."* I agree with Dr. Peale, but I think he left one item off his list. Anyone facing cancer needs *three* things, not two. My advice would be, "Get yourself a good doctor, a good God, and *good friends."* My friends helped me keep my balance and kept me from falling. Their words, kindnesses, and prayers sustained and comforted me while giving me strength. I cannot thank them enough.

If you are one of the 192,280 men diagnosed with prostate cancer this year, let me be the first to welcome you to the club you never wanted to join. You are now my brother.

> *"From now until the end of the world, we and*
> *it shall be remembered. We few, we Band of Brothers.*
> *For he who sheds his blood with me shall be my brother."*
>
> King Henry V
>
> William Shakespeare

# A Note about the Journal Entries

This book contains several journal entries taken from my daily account of this battle with prostate cancer. I wrote the first entry, *Day 1*, within two hours of my diagnosis.

I strategically placed other entries throughout the book to illustrate important points and give a personal, behind-the-scenes look at the disease, its treatment, and recovery. The emotions expressed are as raw as they are real. They are not intended to be mile markers for your own personal journey, but rather to give you some idea of the emotions you may feel while navigating this illness.

———

# THE CLUB YOU NEVER WANTED TO JOIN

# CHAPTER 1

## Getting the news – *then what?*

## *Day 1*

*"You've got cancer."*

Dr. Price said it in a very matter-of-fact tone. No sugarcoated, *"I have some bad news for you…"* Nothing to wash it down. Bad news, served straight up without a garnish.

I could hear Charlotte choking back tears. I couldn't look at her. I suppressed a strong urge to vomit. We spent the next five minutes discussing the Gleason Grading Scale, success rates, surgery, and what happens "after." Then we stumbled out into the bright, fluorescent-lit hallway and walked like zombies toward the bank of gunmetal gray elevators.

The doors slammed shut behind us with a metallic clank, like the sound of prison cell. She cried softly and hugged me so tightly it gave me the impression she was afraid I might float away. My body felt like lead. I wasn't going anywhere.

*"It'll be OK,"* I said.

I didn't know who I was trying to convince.

———

Groucho Marx said he would never join a club that would have him as a member. Groucho had prostate cancer perfectly pegged—welcome to the club you never wanted to join.

First, you should know it's not a terribly exclusive club. According to the American Cancer Society, some 192,280 men will be diagnosed with prostate cancer this year. It hits every stratum of society and about one in six men will get the disease in their lifetime. How it affects you depends a little on luck, some on science, and a lot on *you*.

Do you know the difference between a mild concussion and a severe concussion? A *mild* concussion is one that happens to *someone else!* You've gone all of your life hearing about cancer. Now it's your turn. Maybe for the first time, you know what a "severe" concussion feels like. It's *awful*. Whatever your PSA level, biopsy report, or Gleason Grade, it is *your* cancer and it is *serious*. Nothing anyone can say will change that.

If you're like most men, the word "cancer" and your name have never appeared together in the same sentence. The idea of *you* being sick, let alone having a life-shattering illness, is so foreign, you're probably feeling as if you're in the middle of a very bad dream. This book is your alarm clock. Don't hit the snooze button; it's time to wake up.

There's something you should know right now:

Your "BC" (Before Cancer) life is officially over. There's nothing you can do about that. It's gone.

This book is all about your "AD" life—your life "After Diagnosis." The land you now inhabit. It's time to look around and get comfortable. You're going to be here for the rest of your life.

Getting past the shock of diagnosis isn't easy. Your mind reels with a million questions and you may have mood swings ranging from depression and despair to total rage. But, I'm here to help you get through it. So take a deep breath, and we'll start the first lesson.

***It's going to be OK.***

Sounds simple, doesn't it? That's because it *is* simple.

How can I—someone who doesn't have the initials MD after his name—say you're going to be all right without knowing *your* particular diagnosis? Easy...*you* will make the difference. You are about to take charge and regain control of your treatment and every decision surrounding it. Make a deal with yourself right now. You are no longer a victim that's been assaulted by an invisible intruder. The defense has left the field. It's time to send in the offense. I'll help you put some points on the board.

Let's walk through five things you can do right now to make your life better:

1. **Realize you aren't going to die in the next fifteen minutes.**
   Take a deep breath and consider this fact: prostate cancer survival rates are very high and your chances are excellent. According to the American Cancer Society:
      * The five-year survival rate is 97 percent.
      * The ten-year survival rate is 79 percent.
      * The fifteen-year survival rate is 57 percent.

Compared to other forms of malignant carcinoma, the prognosis for prostate cancer is really very good. It is nearly 100 percent survivable if detected early. The disease is diagnosed every 2.76 minutes and it knows someone in every field of endeavor, from punks (Joey Ramone) to poets (Robert Frost), and politicians (Rudy Giuliani) to pundits (David Brinkley). Robert De Niro, Joe Torre, Johnny Unitas, Robert Goulet, Frank Zappa, and thousands more, all have experienced prostate cancer.

Prostate cancer is the most common cancer in American men. It is the second-leading cause of cancer death among men (lung cancer is number one). According to the American Cancer Society, approximately 27,360 men will die from the disease this year.

African-American men have the highest prostate cancer incidence and mortality in the world. In fact, African-American men are twice as likely to die from it as other men with prostate cancer. Asian men have the lowest incidence of prostate cancer. Researchers haven't determined why there seems to be an ethnic variance, but diet may play a role.

The greatest risk of developing prostate cancer begins at age fifty in white men with no family history of the disease and at age forty for African-American men. Risk increases with age, but there appears to be no "peak" age for developing prostate cancer. It can happen at any time to anyone.

2. **Know all you can know.**

Learn as much as possible about your disease. There is a lot of excellent information out there, so much, in fact, that it can be overwhelming. The "bible" on prostate cancer is *A Primer on Prostate Cancer: The Empowered Patient's Guide* by Stephen B. Strum and Donna Pogliano. This detailed, well-researched book is a must-have for anyone facing prostate cancer. It will probably tell you *more* than you want to know. The only downside is that it is very medical (going from basic diagnosis and treatment all the way through different approaches of chemotherapy).

Hundreds of books have been written about prostate cancer. Some are good; some aren't so good. There's even a "For Dummies" book about prostate cancer that includes some useful information, but it didn't give me all I needed. I wanted to know what to expect from a patient's point of view.

And of course, there are hundreds of Web sites. Type the words "prostate cancer" into any search engine and you'll be hit with thousands of references. My favorite? WebMD (www.webmd.com). The postings on the prostate cancer message board are informative, educational, and enlightening. The "brothers" on this board will answer your specific questions about anything related to the illness. Another excellent resource is *Prostate Pointers* (www.prostatepointers.org). There is a complete list in the back of this book, but these have more than enough information to get you started on our educational journey.

3. **Turn on the Bat Signal.**

Remember the old *Batman* TV series? When Commissioner Gordon needed the Caped Crusader, he would flip on the "Bat Signal" to get help immediately. We have an improved version today, though you may not think of it as the Bat Signal. It's called the Internet.

Once you've gotten past the shock of diagnosis, put the word out to your family, friends, and business associates. Don't forget you're now a member of a very large club. You probably know someone who knows someone who has gone through (or is going through) what you're facing. Remember, prostate cancer is the number one diagnosed cancer among all men. Chances are good that you have a friend who can help you find a great surgeon, consider your options, or lend moral support. The world is a big place and there are plenty of people who can help you find your way around. They just have to know you need help. Let your "Bat Signal" light up the Internet sky on Facebook, Twitter, MySpace, or your personal blog, and the future will look a lot brighter.

4.  **Take a time out.**

    Admit it. You were surprised by your diagnosis. We all are. Even if you are a confirmed pessimist, you just aren't ready for the words, *"You've got cancer."* No one is that pessimistic or that prepared.

    If you didn't arrange a follow-up visit with your urologist when you were first diagnosed, pick up the phone right now and make your next appointment. Why? You'll want to ask the questions you were too stunned to ask when you heard that life-changing news (you'll find sample questions in chapter 4).

    Next, call your boss. Take a couple of days off and start your homework. Go to the library or bookstore, or do some online research. Start filling in the holes in your prostate cancer knowledge and make a list of what you want to know. The goal is to identify your options and learn more about what you're facing. Prostate cancer has blown you right out of your comfort zone. The only way to regain any semblance of

## What's the big idea?

Your first reaction to your diagnosis will probably be that you have to act fast. Unless your urologist tells you to hop up on the table because they have an OR waiting, don't rush your decision. Prostate cancer has the reputation of being one of the slowest growing cancers. Take a deep breath and do a little research. Talk with different doctors as well as friends and family. Then, and only then, make the decision that's right for you. One more thing... don't look back after making your choice. The future is all about recovery, not regret.

comfort is to understand this disease so you can move on to the next step: making an informed decision.

Is a traditional "open" prostatectomy right for you? How about radiation or cryosurgery? Have you considered laparoscopic surgery? What do you think about "watchful waiting"? It's an option too. You could decide not to decide and perform routine PSA tests to ensure the cancer doesn't progress. These are all choices your urologist can help you make. The important thing is that you understand your options, and make the decision that's right for you.

For me, the decision was relatively simple. I reasoned that "watchful waiting" just wasn't an option. I didn't want to look continually over my shoulder to see if my cancer was advancing or retreating. I wanted it out. I wanted it out, *now*.

Did I like the choices I was given? Hell, no. But, I believed the best chance of getting cancer out of my life was to have it surgically removed. I didn't like the potential side effects of incontinence and impotence, but I was more comfortable facing those inconveniences than the chance my cancer might spread into the rest of my body.

*"Dead men don't have sex,"* I told myself. *"Move on."*

One option you certainly have is the opportunity to consider other physicians. The key here is to be entirely comfortable with your doctor. You need someone you can relate to and trust. Communication is critical. If you don't feel as if you can ask or tell your doctor anything, then it's probably time to find someone else. You also need to be confident in his or her abilities. If you are at all unsure, research your physician through online databases and check out his or her experience in this field. I'm not suggesting you become a stalker. However, you want to know as much as you can about the person that's going to have such a huge impact on your life.

### 5. Put a face on your enemy.

Prostate cancer doesn't usually signal before it strikes. Detection is extremely difficult without testing. It's almost an "invisible" invader. In all likelihood, you didn't feel sick before you were diagnosed. Now that you have it, it's unlikely that you can think of much else besides being sick.

I don't know about you, but I have a hard time fighting things I can't see. That's why I named my cancer. "Karl" became my enemy from the minute I spoke his unholy name. From that point forward, my mission was clear: Find Karl. **Kill Karl.** Remove Karl from my life.

Finding Karl was easy. I outsourced that job to my doctors at Urology Associates of North Texas. Killing Karl gave *me* a goal. It gave me a purpose. It gave me my first step. It was a simple thing—just putting a name to the unknown. Once I began my homework and put a mental "face" on my enemy, I felt better. Naming Karl was my first step toward survival. Sure, it was a baby step, but beating this illness takes a million of them. Just keep in mind that each one gets you a little closer to home.

## What you should remember at this point:

1. Your survival chances are excellent.
2. Learn all you can.
3. Get the word out.
4. Take some time off.
5. Put a face on your enemy.

## Day 2

I have cancer.

I've decided to name my cancer. I can't explain why, but I believe if I can name it, I can see it. If I can see it, I can identify it. If I can see it and identify it, I can kill it. My cancer's name is **Karl.** When I get over the shock of having Karl, I am

### What's the big idea?

Get comfortable. You need to become comfortable with your physician AND your disease. Online research is a great way to help you feel more at ease. Begin by checking out your physician and (if appropriate) his or her medical group. You want to know all you can know about the people who are going to have a lasting impact on your life. The more you know, the better you will feel. They say knowledge is power. You want to be as powerful as possible when you make your decisions. It will help you take the edge off your diagnosis and make a better informed (and less stressful) decision.

going to hunt him down and kill him. It will be *Apocalypse Now* in my prostate. The surgeon will travel up the river of my insides and terminate Karl with extreme prejudice.

*Hasta la vista, Karl!*

I don't expect Karl to go peacefully. He won't. A lot depends on what Karl has planned and where he's traveled. A lot more depends on whether the assassin I'm sending to kill him is having a good day or a bad day. Is my guy in the "ZONE"? I hope so.

*"What scares you the most?"* I asked Charlotte last night.

*"That you'll die."*

*"So that's your main fear. That I'll die?"*

She nodded.

*"What's your biggest fear?"* she asked.

*"That I'll live and my sex life will die."*

Boy, did that sound petty. OK, so I come from the shallow end of the gene pool. Sue me. I want it ALL. I want to LIVE and I want my life back.

That's right, Karl. Watch your ass. I WANT MY LIFE BACK. What RIGHT do you have to take that from me? What did I ever do to you? I am going to beat you. I am going to live. Someday, I will be able to say I am a cancer survivor. And like every survivor, I will have a story to tell. My story will be all about how I KICKED KARL'S ASS and lived to tell about it.

———

# CHAPTER 2

# Why me?

## *Beating the odds without beating yourself*

## *Day 4*

We met with one of the surgeons we were considering. We waited over an hour, but when he arrived, he was good at answering our questions. We came prepared; books from Barnes & Noble and a lot of online research helped us ask a lot of questions, some good, some not so good.

He went over the pathology report. Here's where I stand. I am a Gleason 6 (3 primary/3 secondary) with a cancer in stage T1c. My last PSA was 2.7.

Since my urologist wasn't recommending any other options, we discussed the merits of open surgery (slice you up like a tuna) and laparoscopic surgery (slice you up like a tuna, but with smaller bites). This surgeon is the "open" guy, but he really convinced us (much to his chagrin) that laparoscopic was a better choice—shorter hospital stay, less blood loss, less time with a catheter and quicker recovery time: four plus weeks versus six plus. Sounded like a deal to me.

Later in the day, I made an appointment with my primary care doctor and friend, Mike Jutras. I wanted to make sure all my guys—urologists, surgeons, primary care physicians—were talking. I didn't want to have a complication and say to myself in ICU, *"Gee, guess I should have told Mike."* I made the appointment using some mystery illness to fly under the radar. I was his last appointment of the day.

I started to apologize for coming in under false pretenses, but he stopped me in my tracks.

"*I know,*" he said as he opened up a folder and showed me my pathology report.

There in glorious black and white was a diagram of my prostate cut into sections where they had taken the biopsy. It looked like an office football pool. The only difference was that instead of "Tech," "UT," or "A&M," the small squares read "Benign" and "Cancer." "*Thanks,*" I thought to myself. "*I'll take the spread on benign and we'll kick cancer's butt. I like these boys when they play at home and the quarterback is healthy.*"

Mike answered the question I asked on day one—"*Why me?*"—by suggesting I ask instead, "*Why am I a miracle?*" Catching cancer in someone my age at this early a stage was truly a miracle.

I'm a lucky man.

———

Why me?

It's the first question we all ask, and it's easy to see why. We live in a society that assigns blame for everything. There's always someone at fault for an unfortunate incident. Even terrorists accept responsibility for their horrific acts, so why not us? It is, after all, *your* cancer. Didn't you do something to cause it?

No, you didn't.

Outside of being born a male, you didn't do anything to earn your prostate cancer. Other than being a guy (or having a family history), the greatest risk factor is age. If you're forty-five or older, you're at risk. Period.

It's really that simple. Young men can get the disease, but the real risk of getting prostate cancer increases with age. More than 70 percent of men diagnosed with prostate cancer are over sixty-five. Early detection through prostate-specific antigen (PSA) screening is allowing about 75 percent of all new cases to be discovered early, and it's dramatically improving survival rates.

You might just be a member of the unlucky gene club. Having a father or brother with the disease <u>doubles</u> your chances of getting it, according to the American Cancer Society. The male sex hormone testosterone also contributes to its growth. Bottom line…no one is really sure how it works. Some men get it. Some men don't.

Why you?

Why *not* you?

The *"why"* isn't really important.

What *is* important is that you don't become overwhelmed by your diagnosis. It's easy to be buried in the avalanche of data and decisions that have taken over your life. All of this has probably left you feeling as if time is running out and thinking you have to plan the rest of your life in the next five minutes. Relax. You don't.

## Are these questions bothering you?

- What does this diagnosis mean for the rest of my life and how much "rest" do I have?
- Will I die?
- Do I need a living will?
- How can I take care of my family?
- How can I afford it?
- Will it affect my job?
- Does it mean my sex life is over?
- Can my marriage survive?

These are great questions and I promise they'll all be answered. But slow down and take it at your own pace. This is a marathon, not a sprint. Save a little for the backstretch.

You must accept the simple fact that there are things in your life you cannot control. Know this: Even the strongest bridge in the world wasn't engineered to hold all the cars that would travel across it in its lifetime *all at once*. You aren't Superman. And you're certainly not the Golden Gate Bridge. You can't do it either.

However, there are plenty of things you *can* do to relieve your stress and get some answers. Take your questions one at a time and recognize you're not an expert. It's time to call in some reinforcements. You're going to need outside help.

## Get some support.

Don't be afraid to admit that your diagnosis is causing a lot of stress in your life. Ask your urologist or physician to recommend a prostate cancer support group. While such a group can't (and shouldn't) take the place of medical advice, it can help guide you through the disease and offer moral support. There's comfort in knowing you're not alone and that plenty of guys are going through the same thing. They may have developed coping skills that could help you. You may even find a prostate cancer brother who can be your guide.

A minister once told me that the saddest conversation he ever had was with a man who was going through a test of almost biblical proportion. His wife was divorcing him, his kid was on drugs, and his job was being phased out thanks to a corporate merger. At the end of the counseling session, the minister asked if he had a close friend to confide in to help share his burden. "No," he said. *"I've spent my life building my career and there never seemed to be time for friendships."*

Friends are always important, but probably never more so than when you're facing a life-changing illness. Reach out to your friends, especially male friends. Their support and encouragement can carry you through. You may be surprised or even overwhelmed at their kindness and generosity.

## Make financial arrangements in advance.

If finances concern you, call your insurance provider and discuss what your policy covers and how much you can expect to pay. Also, talk with both your doctor's and the hospital's business offices about their payment policies. If you don't have insurance, talk with them about arranging a payment plan in advance of your treatment.

Regardless of your approach, prostate cancer isn't an inexpensive disease. Depending on the illness' severity, it can cost five to six figures for treatment. If you work for a large company, consult the human resources department and make sure you fully understand your health insurance coverage. You need to know how much out-of-pocket expense you can expect and how to handle the paperwork. Communication is critical here. If you can get them involved in your fight against cancer, you'll be better equipped for the battle.

## Talk it over with your boss.

Depending on your relationship with your employer, you may want to discuss your prostate cancer at this point. Talk about any concerns you have and make sure you understand the company policy surrounding medical leave.

Thanks to HIPPA, your employer won't ask a lot of questions, so you're free to volunteer as much information as you're comfortable giving. It's up to you, but I encourage keeping your employer as informed as possible. Why? You can count on human nature. We (OK, most of us) instinctively want to help people. Give your boss a chance to show some support, and accept whatever is offered.

Be up front about needing time off. No one can accurately predict how long you'll be away from the job—a lot depends on what kind of work

### What's the big idea?

One way to conquer your fear is to know as much about your disease as humanly possible. When you know more, you fear less. Arrange for a few days off and do some homework. Go to the public library and get online. You can find plenty of information just by plugging the words "prostate cancer" into Google or some other search engine. Learn all you can and then get back to your doctor with a list of specific questions. The chances are excellent that the knowledge you gain will help increase your confidence in beating this disease.

you can do (for example, you won't be able to lift anything heavier than ten pounds until six weeks after surgery). If you keep the communication lines open and honest, most employers will be understanding and helpful. If your boss knows what to expect, there will be less chance of disappointment or disagreement in the future. An informed employer can be one of your strongest allies and biggest supporters.

One tip you may find useful here, since you really *don't* know how long you'll be away from the job, is that it's probably best to *under* promise and *over* deliver to give yourself a cushion. I'm not suggesting you lie, but I advocate giving yourself plenty of time to recuperate. Right now, you don't know how much time you'll need. Allow yourself a little "wiggle room" on this one and you'll come back to work mentally and physically ready. Everyone, including your boss, will be a lot happier.

## Keep the lines of communication open.

Be open and honest with your spouse (we'll spend an entire chapter on this). Tell her what you are thinking, ask what she is feeling, and don't be afraid to be afraid. This is new territory for you both, so don't be surprised if you don't have all the answers. You'll have individual questions, as well as "couple" questions. Consider meeting with your urologist or physician as a couple to gather more information.

There are plenty of great books covering virtually every topic for the "after" part of this disease. You can find information on everything from loss of intimacy to dealing with impotence and incontinence. The more *both* of you understand about prostate cancer and how it can affect you as a *couple,* the easier it is to handle. You don't have to discuss everything all at once, but be open and honest about sharing the things that concern you. You've probably never needed each other more than you do right now. Keep the conversation going even when you're having trouble expressing your thoughts. Just keep talking and the words will come.

## Be open to miracles.

It's time you started keeping your eyes open for the miracle. I know it sounds corny, but it can do a lot to lift your spirits. Every diagnosis is different, but there is an excellent chance you are a lot luckier than you think. In a perverse way, you truly are the "chosen one," the one out of six guys that have the disease—a disease, don't forget, that is nearly 100 percent survivable if detected early.

Instead of torturing yourself with "Why *me?*" ask simply, "*Why am I the miracle?*" The answer might surprise you. It did me.

# *Day 4, Continued*

Charlotte and I decided to tell Cole. She busied herself in the kitchen so she wouldn't cry. I sat down with him choosing the pull-the-Band-Aid-off-quick approach that been done to me.

"Cole, I have something to tell you."

"Yeah."

"I have cancer."

He doubled over and began to sob to the point of wailing. I sat down beside him on the couch; I held him and reassured him that I would be OK. Mike, "Dr. Mike," after all, had just said I was a "miracle." I think I convinced him that I would be all right. We went through everything we knew up to that point and he seemed comforted by the fact that I hadn't sugarcoated anything.

## What's the big idea?

One of the first questions your employer is going to want answered is "When will you be back at work?" If you're completely honest, you really don't have an answer to that question. Depending on the type of job you have, you could be back in some capacity in a couple of weeks. For some guys, it takes four to six weeks or longer (in case of some postoperative complication). My advice is to give yourself some room when responding. If your physician says you can expect to return to work in four weeks, tell your boss five. If the doctor says six weeks, say seven. It's much better to give the appearance of returning to work early rather than late.

Guess I need to work on my bedside manner.

———

Is there a miracle out there for you? Do you *want* one? Wherever you are in your spiritual journey, you can find comfort in being open to the possibility.

What is a miracle really? It is hope made real. Even if it's nothing more than a glimpse of something better, you have to be looking if you're ever going to see it. You may find it in a new treatment, a doctor you connect with, or a quicker recovery time. Whatever it is—and I'm betting you'll see some along your journey—you won't recognize them if you aren't looking. Lift your head up and be aware of what's going on around you. Even with a cancer diagnosis, there are still a lot of good things going on in the world. Some of them may just rub off on you.

## What you should remember at this point:
1. You didn't cause your cancer.
2. You don't have to have all of the answers today.
3. Accept there are things you can't control.
4. Ask for help.
5. Find the miracle.

# *Day 12*

Does God put people in front of you for a reason?

That's what I wondered as we continued our Christmas shopping today. Barnes & Noble. That's where I saw him, sitting alone at a small table beside a videotape player with a continuous loop of his life story on one-half-inch VHS tape. Here, before me, in all this holiday hustle, was a Holocaust survivor—tanned, elderly, hair neatly combed, looking nothing like the little boy who survived the horrors of Auschwitz. Now, he was just a nice-looking elderly gentleman signing his book. His book about survival.

*"How do people do that?"* I thought to myself. *"How can you survive something so evil? So deadly."* Then it hit me. He DID survive. He DID live to tell the story. Here he sat no more than two feet in front of me. No worse for the wear—that is if you don't count the nightmares, or the crude number tattooed on his forearm. He came through.

Does God put people in front of you for a reason? Was this my road sign? My Auschwitz angel? I guess it's all in the interpretation. My gut told me that this guy survived Auschwitz for a whole lot of reasons. Maybe one of them was ME.

Whatever the reason we crossed paths that day—cosmic or commercial—it made me feel a little better, like my cancer wasn't nearly as big. It made my problem feel small, a little less significant.

I know I have no right to compare myself to someone like a death camp survivor. But there is a reason for everything. Maybe, like other survivors of unspoken horrors, I can tell the story. Give someone else hope. If that's the plan and that's the outcome, then I can begin to see the logic in all of this.

———

# CHAPTER 3

## The c word

### Day 18

The c word.

It's been brought to my attention that we don't like the c word around here. It scares us. It depresses us. It pisses us off. We flat just don't like it.

Of course, the c word I'm referring to is: "cancer."

That being said, it really doesn't bother me as much as some others. It scares me. But the word itself seems to have adopted an almost magical power. It changes people's perception of you and you have to give it credit; it's one hell of a conversation stopper.

I used the c word today in a meeting with our financial planner. He was droning on about the benefits of one mutual fund over another, ten-year histories, and so on. He asked me what I thought about his recommendations for our future.

*"Well, a lot has changed since we first developed our financial plan,"* I opened. *"Now that I have CANCER, my perspective has changed."*

Silence. You might even say "dead" silence.

At lunch, Charlotte told me she didn't like me talking *"like that."* She explained that when I did, it gave her the impression that I had "given up" and that there was "no future, only 'now.'" I tried to reassure her that I haven't given up. Why would I? But my perspective HAD changed since being diagnosed.

I still subscribe to magazines and buy green bananas, but I'm not that keen on thirty-year municipal bonds. Life is short. Karl, that miserable bastard, has taught me that painful lesson.

So I guess I'll relegate the c word to Web postings with my PCa brothers and a couple of friends who've joined the club. They don't like the c word either, but they've earned the right to use it.

———

Our ancestors thought some words were *so* powerful that people were forbidden to speak them. We're not so different, you and me. We've evolved and advanced. Gone from caves to condos, but we have words like that, too. **CANCER** is one of them.

There's no mistaking the power of that word. I'll bet you'll never forget the first time you saw it on a piece of paper with your name beside it. Remember how you felt when you read your biopsy report?

Whether you like it or not, you now carry the big red **C** on your forehead. Your friends—even your enemies—now have a label for you. You're the guy with *"cancer."* It's not just something you have to get used to. Everyone you know has to get used to it too.

Ever been to a modern art museum and seen a mobile? The funny thing about mobiles is that if you move one part, everything else moves in relation to it. That's cancer. Cancer rearranges everything and everybody it touches. In addition to your life being upside down, you have to realize that all of your relationships are being affected by this disease.

Are you married? You may notice a change almost immediately after diagnosis. According to researchers, the good news is that if you had a good marriage *before* your cancer, you stand a good chance of having one after cancer. I happen to believe you can come out with an even stronger relationship.

The question of whether cancer is a factor in divorce is just now getting the study it deserves. It's a tough one. With a national divorce rate hovering around 50 percent, the role cancer may or may not play in a breakup is hard to determine.

I won't lie to you. Surviving prostate cancer can be like enduring one hundred automobile accidents. This long strange trip will take its toll on you. In some cases, that toll is a marriage. How do you keep your cancer from crashing your relationship? Buckle your seatbelts and follow these directions.

## Face your fear.

It's OK to be afraid. Everyone has some fear of the unknown and there are plenty of "unknowns" in your life today. You're afraid your cancer might kill you. You're worried your sex life is over. You may just be afraid of being afraid. Your spouse is just as scared. The only way you're going to get through this is to get through it together.

Talking about your feelings isn't just something "sensitive" guys do on Oprah. Get that idea out of your head. No one is suggesting you start channeling Dr. Phil, but it's time you opened up and talked about your cancer and the things that are bothering you. You'll probably find that you share many of the same concerns. When you face your fears together, you're stronger. That strength can keep you both headed in the right direction and help you stare down the worries that are holding you back.

# *Day 21*

I'm a planner. That's what I do. I plan and I plan to leave as little to chance as I possibly can. It's an unpleasant trait, but like this cancer that's trying to kill me, it's something I live with.

This morning I prepared instructions for my funeral. Not a cheery thought at 7:30 a.m., but one I tackled all the same.

My plan is to let someone close to me know about the envelope with instructions and use it to guide them if something happens. Not that I'm anticipating that, but planners plan and that's what I was doing—planning, trying to give Charlotte one less thing to do on possibly the hardest day of her life.

I made a list of the usual things—minister, music, Bible verse, etc. My first wish was simple.

"Keep it brief," said the instructions.

Of all the wishes I expressed, brevity was the most important to me. If the unthinkable happens, I want whoever shows up to get a few hopeful words and a song—get in and get out. Like a NASCAR pit stop on the eternal highway, no use hanging around. I won't be.

---

## Accept your anger.

Have you ever seen the movie *Network*? The main character is a television news anchor named Howard Beal. Howard loses it during a newscast and shouts into the camera, *"I'm mad as hell and I'm not going to take it anymore!"* Sound like you? Has cancer made you mad as hell? What are *you* going to do about it? You certainly don't have to lie there and take it. But it's probably best if you don't go nuts on national TV. Accept that you're mad and do something positive with that anger.

You could start by adjusting your expectations. Deal with things you can manage and don't worry about the rest. If your "to do" list is ten items long, pare it down to two or three and work on the other items later. A sense of accomplishment can go a long way toward reducing your anger and relieving your stress.

Just taking your mind off things can help. Do you enjoy sports? How about fishing, hiking, or biking—anything that gives your mind a break from the disease can help relieve your anxiety and rage. Remember, it's natural to be angry; it's just healthier to find a positive outlet for it. Your family and friends will thank you and so will your body.

## Ask "What if?"

People make mistakes, even doctors, surgeons, and the folks in white coats in laboratories. Could there have been a mistake in your pathology report? It's possible and it's worth asking about.

You may want a second opinion. That's OK and, in many cases, your insurance will even cover the cost. Most doctors, however, will strongly advise you against having another biopsy. The procedure isn't pleasant and it can take your body up to six weeks to heal after the exam.

So what do you do? My advice is to ask your urologist these questions:

- "Is it possible there has been a mistake?"
- "Are you 100 percent certain these results belong to me?"

It sounds so obvious, but simple questions like these that can cause even the most harried physician to pause and consider the possibility that an error may have been made. Sometimes, that's all it takes. You may like the outcome. You may not. At least, you'll have the confidence that comes from asking the question.

## Discuss your depression.

Anger has a best friend named depression, and you can find them hanging out together all the time. If you're angry—really angry—about your prostate cancer, there's an excellent chance you also have feelings of despair. These feelings can be mild, moderate, or even severe. Different people react in different ways.

A good way to deal with your depression is to talk about it with someone. That someone could be your spouse or significant other. Maybe your priest, pastor, or rabbi. It could be a close friend or your family doctor. Just remember, you can't deal with it if you don't talk about it.

It's wise to help the people in your life understand you so they can support you. If family and friends can put themselves

**What's the big idea?**

If you have any of these symptoms for two weeks or longer, seek professional help immediately:

* Changes in appetite or weight
* Changes in sleep patterns
* Restlessness or decreased activity noticeable to your family, friends, or co-workers
* Loss of energy or a sense of feeling "tired" all the time
* Feelings of worthlessness or guilt
* Thoughts of death or suicide

into your shoes, they can do a much better job of helping you through this. There are prostate cancer support groups that do an excellent job of providing the moral support that so many of us need. Ask your urologist to recommend a prostate cancer support group and then attend one of the sessions.

WebMD has an online prostate cancer chat room where you can get immediate answers to your questions and plenty of encouragement from people just like you. Check out the Web site (www.webmd.com) for days and times.

# *Day 22*

I'm depressed.

Here's what's worrying me. What if the cancer really isn't contained in the prostate? What if they open me up only to find they made a mistake and it has spread to God knows where? *Then what?*

One of life's ironies would be that I would *immediately* bargain my way back to accepting prostate cancer and that would be a *good* thing. Jeez, the waiting on this is driving me crazy. RIP THIS BASTARD OUT OF ME BEFORE IT DOES ANY MORE DAMAGE!

Instead, I get appointment times a week or two or three weeks later. Watching. Waiting. Feeling. Wondering.

Did that twinge I felt when I rolled over last night mean anything? What's that? A lump? No, can't be…just my imagination. Doctor said it was all contained. It's a slow-moving cancer. Not going anywhere fast. Then again, neither am I.

Here's the deal, Doc. You get this son of a bitch out of me and I'll tell you the difference between fast and slow. Would *you* wait?

———

## Keep your eyes on the prize.

You are fighting so many battles right now, but there is only one fight you absolutely, positively must win: the battle to make yourself cancer free.

Nothing else matters. Hell, nothing else even comes close. Whatever you do, whatever curves this disease throws at you, do not lose sight of this goal. It is the single-most important thing in your life right now.

### What you should remember at this point:
1. Face your fear.
2. Accept your anger.
3. Ask "What if?"
4. Discuss your depression.
5. Keep your eyes on the prize.

# Day 23

My friends don't know what to think of me and this "thing" I have. If I were honest with myself, I'd say I don't either. WHO am I now? WHAT is this now? What happens next? Who the hell knows?

Tony Comparin called the night before and invited me to Monday's Mavericks game— not a terribly unusual event—but one I suspect was motivated more out of concern than camaraderie. I took him up on it.

Game time.

Tony picked me up first. Alone in the car, a brief uneasy silence between us, we made our way through a Colleyville autumn to pick up Jay and Rick. We headed down the back road toward their homes. The pecan trees were tossing leaves at us as if we were suddenly swept up in a tickertape parade. Soon they'd be bare. Stripped of their dignity and reduced to their essence. We had a lot in common that evening. There were no giant Macy's-type balloons in this autumn parade, just two guys heading out to a ball game. The question came.

*"So, I heard about your deal,"* Tony said.

*"Yeah, it's a deal all right,"* I mused.

*"So, did they catch it early?"* Tony must have had some medical training in his accounting courses at UT. Memo to myself: I have to look into that.

*"Yeah, they caught it early. At least that's what they tell me."*

*"Well, that's good."*

Congratulations! You've found the good in this dilemma in only two questions. Care to move on to the bonus round? Tony did.

*"Yeah, it's good because they usually don't. If they'd checked me out a couple of years from now when I turn fifty, it might have been too late,"* I said sounding hopeful.

*"How'd they catch it?"* he pushed a little.

*"Routine blood test,"* I mumbled, my shorthand getting better with each telling. *"My PSA was high and they sent me in for a biopsy. Tests came back positive."*

*"When you having surgery?"* he asked, avoiding eye contact with me.

*"I should know Wednesday. At least that's what I hope."*

We pulled up to Jay's house—the usual handshakes and greetings, small talk, basketball talk, business talk. Normal. A cold beer and a hot dog and I was better by tip-off.

Charlotte was right to encourage me to get out.

*"You'll have a lot of time around the house. Go!"* she said.

I'm glad I did.

———

# CHAPTER 4

# MD Doesn't Mean Minor Deity

## Day 25

Charlotte and I met with Dr. David Lee this afternoon, and we were so anxious to see him we arrived forty-five minutes early for our appointment.

Dr. Lee is an affable, young (early thirties) laparoscopic surgeon about five feet eight with short black hair. He has a wife, two kids, and lives in our neighborhood. He answered my questions as if I were the only patient he had that day (I wasn't) and he was candid about his experience and my projected outcome.

We came prepared. I had a full page of questions (single-spaced) that ranged from *"How many LRPs have you done?"* (about one hundred) to *"Have you ever lost a patient?"*

*"Have I ever lost a patient? You mean, during a prostate operation?"* he asked.

*"Yes, during a prostate operation. I'm sorry to ask, but I have to know for my own peace of mind,"* I answered.

*"No...no...no..."* he said, the volume of voice decreasing with each *"no."*

*"Good. I was hoping you would say that. Charlotte was hoping you'd say that too."*

*"There was this time...,"* he added, the candor showing through. He described an experience as a resident where an older woman died during a kidney tumor operation. It had nothing to do with a male...or a prostate... but I was surprised and impressed with his willingness to tell the story to someone who was "interviewing" him for a job—the most important hire I've ever done.

After making sure Dr. Lee had answered all of Charlotte's questions, I moved in for the close.

I had something I had wanted to ask throughout the interview, but I didn't know if it was appropriate. After spending some time with this man...this surgeon...this person...who would pretty much dictate the rest of my life, I couldn't help myself. I had ONE MORE question. A question that began with a statement.

*"Dr. Lee, I want you to know something,"* I said.

*"Yes, Mr. Hill."*

*"If we do this with you, I want you to know there will be a lot of people praying for me."* I paused. My throat muscles contracted as my tear ducts filled almost to capacity. I took a deep breath and continued.

*"They'll be praying for you too,"* I said, hurrying to get the words out before I lost it.

Silence.

Dr. Lee looked at me as if I had just given him the two-day forecast—sunny and clear with a high in the mid-seventies.

What was he thinking? What would he say? I didn't have to wait long for an answer.

*"Mr. Hill, I believe God has given me a gift to do this surgery and I will do it to the best of my ability,"* he said, calm, confident, secure in his knowledge, and strong in his belief.

I stood up, having regained my composure. I reached out and shook his hand. I turned to Charlotte and nodded an approval.

*"Dr. Lee,"* I said, *"you're our guy."*

He smiled. Charlotte smiled. Maybe even God smiled.

It was a good day.

———

If you're like me, you grew up with a healthy respect for authority. You know who I'm talking about—teachers, preachers, doctors, and police, people who told you what to do, which you did without questioning. There is nothing wrong with respecting authority, but there's nothing wrong with *questioning* authority either.

You don't have to be a jerk about it, but you also don't have to go along blindly with everything somebody in a white coat tells you. Sure, they understand your disease. But these guys often disagree among themselves on the proper course of treatment. Remember, nobody knows more about *you* than *you*. My hope is that you make informed decisions. Listen carefully to what the experts say. Decide what is right for you. And never look back.

You're going to meet some amazing people on your journey down this prostate path. They all have something to contribute to your recovery, but don't mistake them for Gods. I say this with deep affection and profound respect for the medical profession. Some of my best friends are doctors.

One of the first things you'll learn is that doctors respond best when asked *direct* questions. My advice is to come to any doctor's appointment prepared with a list of questions. It doesn't have to be nice, neat, or typewritten—you won't be graded—just enough to help you keep your thoughts straight and avoid forgetting anything. Take a tape recorder if you're not a note-taking kind of guy (most doctors don't consider it an intrusion, but tell them what you're doing as a courtesy).

Ask anything and everything you want to know. Nothing is out of bounds; this is your life you're talking about. If you're worried a question might offend your physician, you may have chosen the wrong guy. I can't stress this enough. You have to establish a comfort zone with your doctor. Communication is critical to your care. This person is going to be a part of your life for a very long time. You're not making a lunch date.

Many surgeons have a "Lone Ranger" attitude. That doesn't mean their bedside manner sucks (*OK, sometimes it does*), but some believe that once they've opened you up and removed your prostate, their job is over. They're ready to climb on their horse and say, "*My work here is done. Let's ride, Tonto!*"

The dirty little secret is that while they're checking out, you're checking in. Your work is really just *beginning*. You have a whole new life ahead of you, and a little help navigating your new body would be nice. Don't expect your surgeon to offer much advice beyond the standard post-op recovery instructions. You're pretty much on your own here.

Once you've crossed the line and decided prostate surgery is right for you, the next critical decision is choosing your surgeon. You can narrow the field by deciding which type of surgery is best for you. Your urologist may or may not suggest anything other than the standard radical prostatectomy. Whatever the recommendation, ask about alternatives.

I chose a robotic-assisted radical laparoscopic prostatectomy (RLRP) rather than the more traditional "open" surgery. I figured that if I was going to have an operation, I might as well be on the cutting edge of what was then new technology! Looking back, I don't regret deciding to go the RLRP route. It worked for me. You have to consider your options and make your mind up about what's best for you.

# *Day 27*

I went in for my pre-op exam today. This wasn't an unpleasant trip, but they ask a lot of questions that put me in the same frame of mind that began my day. Everything I experienced centered around "What happens if?" At one point, I found myself in a small waiting room with about four chairs. An elderly man and woman were seated four feet from me filling out the questionnaire.

The man was obviously the "patient." He couldn't see well enough to read and his lack of hearing complicated things for both of them. She decided to read the questionnaire to him and fill it out herself. But she was overwhelmed by the form and put off by the questions it asked.

*"HAVE YOU EVER BEEN SEXUALLY ABUSED?"* she shouted even though her husband was one foot away from her.

*"What?"* he answered. The volume went up a notch.

*"HAVE YOU EVER BEEN SEXUALLY ABUSED? IS ANYONE ABUSING YOU NOW?"* she continued in a voice that bordered on shouting. I'd rank the sound level a ten on the *Spinal Tap* amplifier scale of eleven.

*"NO!"* he hollered back at her.

*"My Lord, would you look at all of these questions,"* she replied. *"I don't know how we'll fill all this out."*

She had mistaken the stack of paper on the clipboard to be a multi-page questionnaire and had ignored the sign on the front that read: "Fill Out <u>One</u> Form, Front and Back." It was obvious she was going to be here awhile. The door opened and the nurse called me back. I escaped within an inch of my sanity.

Plenty of prodding and poking followed. Blood—lots of blood. Urine— *"Please give me a sample midstream,"* the nurse instructed. *"You do know what I mean by midstream, don't you?"* she asked. I assured her I was continent and capable of understanding her.

Blood pressure (123/82) followed. An EKG and a chest X-ray wrapped up the visit. In and out in about an hour. Kind of like EyeMasters without the dilation drops.

That evening, I had a call from our new minister. Funny, he doesn't know my name on Sunday, but he knows who I am now. Cancer does that to people. Suddenly, you become someone. It's as if you stand out from the crowd. *"Oh yeah,"* they must say to themselves, *"you're the cancer guy."* Kind of like visual shorthand. Whatever it is, it must work.

The conversation was brief. I had things to do. I was preparing to get "in the ZONE" for this surgery I'll face in three days. I have to be focused, positive, ready. I'm going to beat this bastard, but I have to get my game face on.

———

Most guys are really good at buying a house or a car, but they don't know anything about selecting a surgeon. In the grand scheme of things, this may be the single biggest decision in your life. Use these questions to help make your decision easier.

# What to Ask Your Surgeon

1. **How many prostatectomies have you done?**

   <u>Tip</u>: Look for a response in the hundreds. If the surgeon you're considering hasn't done more than one hundred of the exact type of surgery you're considering, keep walking. I'll admit it doesn't bother some guys. I've talked to folks who were the third and fourth patients of a particular surgeon and everything went fine. You just wouldn't find me hopping up on the table.

2. **Where did you go to school and how long have you been with this medical group?**

   <u>Tip</u>: Find out everything you can about your surgeon: where he interned, how he came to this particular field of study, what led him to this specific medical group. You want information to expand your comfort zone. You may even discover you have friends in common or like the same things. You're trying to establish some kind of a connection here. For example, does he play golf? What will this surgery do to *your* golf game? How soon after surgery will you be able to tee 'em up? Why is this important? Do you want your surgeon operating on a "patient" or "Bob, the guy with an April golf trip to Pebble Beach?" Try to make a connection. Trust me. It *does* make a difference.

3. **Have you ever lost a patient in surgery?**

   <u>Tip</u>: Don't be afraid to ask this question. I was concerned I might piss off my surgeon, but that didn't stop me. I was relieved by his response and his honesty.

4. **What's the typical hospital stay?**

   <u>Tip</u>: Unless there are complications, most will have you home within twenty-four hours of a laparoscopic procedure. You're looking at about a three-day hospital stay following the traditional "open" prostatectomy.

5. **Would you describe the surgery for me?**

   Tip: Get specifics. You want to know what you'll have to do beforehand, what will happen during the surgery, and what you can expect after it's over.

6. **What will you remove and why?**

   Tip: Your surgeon will hedge his bets on this one. He will tell you he won't know until he gets inside, but no surgeon operates without a game plan. Your biopsy gave him a good idea of what he's going to find. Ask him what he "typically" removes and why, and what that means to your ultimate recovery.

7. **How long will I be in surgery?**

   Tip: A good rule of thumb is about three hours.

8. **What's your success rate as defined by continence, ability to achieve erections, and nonrecurrence of the disease?**

   Tip: He'll talk in percentages. For example, he might say, "Sixty percent are fully continent within six months and the remaining 40 percent are continent within a year"—something like that. The erection question is trickier. The success rate here is usually based on your past sexual history (i.e., how were your erections before?), and he'll express the recovery time in months, sometimes years. Don't let this discourage you. They all do this.

## What's the big idea?

Be very clear on the directions you give your surgeon. My guy wanted to do everything possible for me to resume a "normal" sex life after surgery, so he was willing to do everything remotely possible to achieve that goal.

I told him my first objective was to be CANCER FREE and there was no second objective. I used a little rhyme to help him remember my request: *"When in doubt, cut it out!"*

We laughed about the goofy rhyme, but we both knew that curing the cancer came first. There was no second.

9. **Will you do a pathological exam of my prostate?**

    <u>Tip</u>: You should get a full pathology report on your prostate, because it's the only way to determine if the cancer has spread. You'll also want to know how long it will take to get back the results. This can take a couple of days or a couple of weeks. You want to know how long you'll have to wait so you don't become overanxious waiting for the phone to ring.

10. **Will you remove the nerve bundles that control erection?**

    <u>Tip</u>: Your surgeon will likely do his best to spare one, if not both, sets of the nerves located on the right and left side of your prostate. What he takes and what he leaves depends entirely on what he finds when he operates and what you've discussed in advance.

11. **What are the chances of recurrence?**

    <u>Tip</u>: He'll be in a better position to answer this question once he sees the pathology report. However, he's already formed some opinion from your biopsy results.

12. **How fast do I need to do something?**

    <u>Tip</u>: Prostate cancer is typically slow growing. It's unlikely he'll hurry you. If surgery isn't required immediately, take some time. Use it to do your homework and make the decision that feels most comfortable.

## What you should remember at this point:
1. Come prepared with a list of questions or a recorder.
2. Choose a surgeon you can really talk to.
3. Make a connection.
4. Give clear directions.
5. Respect authority but don't let it bully you.

# Day 28

We went to see Dr. Lee for the last time before my surgery. I had only a couple of questions and a couple of requests.

My requests?

*"First rule is get the cancer. We can deal with anything else later,"* I told Dr. Lee.

*"Anything else?"* he asked.

*"Yes,"* I answered. *"Remember this: when in doubt…cut it out!"*

He smiled. *"OK, Mr. Hill, I'll try and remember."*

I told him that I was ready.

*"I want you to know I'm in 'the Zone,'"* I said.

*"Good, mental attitude is very important. It's good to be in the Zone,"* he said.

*"Yeah, but I want you in the Zone too,"* I replied.

*"OK,"* he said with a laugh. *"I'll be in the Zone."*

God, how I hope he is. I hope he is in the Zone so deep that he can't see anything else except my cancer. I want him to zero in on Karl like a laser-guided missile and terminate that bastard. Get him out of me…for good.

———

# NOBODY LOOKS GOOD IN A HOSPITAL GOWN

# CHAPTER 5

# Finding the "Zone":

## *Mentally preparing yourself for surgery*

## *Day 30*

It's been one month since I heard the news, "You've got cancer." A lot can happen in thirty short days. In that time, I've:

- scared the crap out of my family;
- found not one, but two excellent laparoscopic radical prostatectomy surgeons;
- told all my family and friends;
- researched my illness to the point of understanding;
- had four doctor appointments;
- wrapped up things at work so I can take off a few days;
- bought "sick" clothes that I absolutely hate—an entire wardrobe of baggy pants, boxer shorts, and comfortable attire; and
- wrangled an earlier surgery date.

Yeah, it's been a busy month.

Tomorrow is "Game Day." The day when I wake up at 4:00 a.m. and travel down dark and silent streets to my appointment with destiny. This day will not be like any other. This day, like all big game days, will have a life-altering outcome. A lot can happen in a single day. Am I ready? I told Dr. Lee I was "in the ZONE" two days ago. Am I ready? Is anyone ever *really* ready?

I think I'm going to have to treat this like the Airborne Rangers in World War II. I'll stand in the doorway with the chute on my back, staring blankly into the dark void, and instinctively jump when the green light goes on.

Will I hesitate? No, I'll jump into that deep and frightening void. All I can hope for is a safe landing on this side of the enemy.

Watch your ass, Karl. Dr. Lee and I are coming to get you.

———

OK, you've weighed the evidence and decided to have surgery. You've determined what type is best for you. You've even chosen a surgeon you can actually talk to, and now you're ready for what comes next. You are ready, aren't you? Almost. It's time to get in the ZONE.

What exactly is the *ZONE?*

It's a positive frame of mind that you must create to stay focused on the only goal that matters: removing cancer from your life. Zones are as unique as snowflakes. How you achieve yours is up to you. The only thing that's really important is that you create one.

I didn't know about the ZONE before I got sick. Looking back, I think I stumbled on to it. I am not, by nature, a peppy, glass-is-half-full kind of guy, but I sensed my survival chances would be better if I could at least convince myself they were good. I reasoned that if I could persuade my mind, my body would follow. It was worth a shot. And I believe it worked for me.

Here are some tips to help you find your ZONE.

## Get Out!

If you've been depressed, it's time to shake it off or get professional help. You need your family and friends to rally around you. It's important to concentrate on what comes next: your complete recovery from prostate cancer. You must develop the attitude that nothing—absolutely nothing—can keep you from achieving that goal.

Take the first step by taking some steps. Exercise is a good way to beat the blues if your doctor says it's OK. Get outside and enjoy the scenery.

Take long walks with your spouse or some friends. Do it early, or do it late. But do it. You'll sleep better and you'll feel stronger.

## Get Fit!

Resolve to eat healthier. You're about to enter a period in your life where it's OK to spoil yourself a little with "comfort" foods. Right now, however, make sure you get your daily supply of fruits, vegetables, and vitamins. Let the food pyramid help you rebuild the temple of your body. Cut back on alcohol; and if you smoke, it's time to quit. I know it sounds a little hard, but it's important to be physically and mentally prepared for this next step.

## Get God!

How's your faith holding up? Are you mad at God?

A friend once told me a story from his early days as a hospital chaplain. He was in the hospital late one night when he heard some noise coming from the chapel. As he made his way down the hall, the sounds became louder.

He carefully opened the door to the small room and peeked inside. There, in the dimly lit chapel, he saw a middle-aged man screaming profanities at the cross. He froze, not knowing if he should go inside and offer comfort or just let the man get it out of his system.

He entered and stood in the back of the room while the man continued his religious rant. Moments later, the man ran out of words and fixed his bloodshot eyes on the young minister.

*"What do you want?"* he challenged.

*"Nothing,"* the minister said.

*"You can't stop me. I have a right, you know?"*

*"It's OK,"* the chaplain reassured. *"He's big enough to take it."*

How are you holding up? Could you use a little help right now? Wherever you are in your spiritual expedition, you may find it reassuring to strengthen your religious ties or reconnect in some meaningful way. Don't be afraid to reach out. It's never too late and it may be just what you need to find your ZONE.

I'm just a backsliding Methodist, but I found a lot of comfort in the 121st Psalm:

> *1 I lift up my eyes to the hills—where does my help come from? 2 My help comes from the LORD, the Maker of heaven and earth. 3 He will not let your foot slip—he who watches over you will not slumber; 4 indeed, he who watches over Israel will neither slumber nor sleep. 5 The LORD watches over you—the LORD is your shade at your right hand; 6 the sun will not harm you by day, nor the moon by night. 7 The LORD will keep you from all harm—he will watch over your life; 8 the LORD will watch over your coming and going both now and forevermore.*

## Get your team behind you!

You're not the only one who needs to get in the ZONE. Your surgeon needs a ZONE of his own. Although many of them have that "Lone Ranger" attitude, it's important to remember that even the Lone Ranger had Tonto. You can help him with his ZONE by maintaining yours. Keep in mind, you've chosen the best man for the job, right? Well, have a little faith in the guy and don't hesitate to show it when you have the opportunity. When someone sees that you have confidence in him, he usually does a better job. Isn't that what you want?

## Get Positive!

Finally, keep a positive attitude. Remember your first lesson? *"It's going to be OK."* It really is. But the only way you can get there is by keeping positive.

Make an effort to take the negative influences out of your life. Avoid negative thinking, negative behavior, negative people...negative everything. It's time to embrace the good things in your life. Look around—and even though you have prostate cancer—you'll be able to find something encouraging. There's a lot to enjoy in the world, but it's only visible to people who open themselves up to it.

1. You must create a ZONE.
2. Turn off everything negative.
3. Get your body, mind, spirit, and friends working together.
4. You're going to beat this thing.

# *Day 30, continued*

Charlotte and I left the office and headed home. We had one of the biggest fights we'd had since I was diagnosed. *"So, what are you thinking you'd like to eat next week?"* she asked. It was a simple question, but it hit me funny.

*"I dunno,"* I mumbled as I threaded my way through traffic. *"Angel hair pasta, stuff that's easy to digest. Dr. Lee said I'd be on a stool softener for a few days."*

*"I was thinking I'd make my poppy seed chicken one day,"* she continued.

*"Yeah, OK,"* I said, not paying much attention.

My response caught her funny and her lip began to quiver. All I could think was how insignificant this line of discussion was when I was facing the toughest battle of my life.

*"What do I want to eat? Hell, I don't know. How about a plate of cancer with a side of chemo?"* I caught myself before the words came out.

We yelled. We argued. The conversation pretty much centered on my feelings that I was headed to a funeral and her feelings that she wasn't helping. I became a little too

## What's the big idea?

You have to "flip the switch" on your attitude from the very beginning. If you're a negative guy, it's time to start thinking positive. If you're a positive guy, you need to be more positive than you've ever been in your life.

I began my fight by telling everyone I would "beat this thing." This self-talk helped me convince myself and encouraged others to stay optimistic. This positive "energy" made a huge difference in my attitude. Create your own ZONE. Fill it with helpful people and constructive thoughts and you'll be amazed at the impact.

self-righteous and a little too pitying. She obsessed about her inability to help me and the despair she was feeling. Is there any good way to deal with something like this? I don't know. What are the rules of engagement in a battle where you could lose your life?

This is something they never showed on *Leave it to Beaver*. I bet Ward never had to discuss chicken and cancer with June.

———

# CHAPTER 6

## What's it *really* like?

### Day 31

We were silent in the car as it made its way through the traffic-free streets toward my date with a surgical robot. What was there to say? We'd covered it all and, besides, neither of us wanted to scare each other any more than we were already scared. Why add to it?

They met us at the front desk—cold, efficient. *"Take a seat,"* was all they said.

Soon we were back in the brightly lit, sterile hospital environment. I changed into the one-size-fits-all hospital gown. I looked like I'd been swallowed by a fashion-challenged monster. I disappeared into the blue-and-gray smock. Maybe they wouldn't find me in there. Maybe it was a "magic" smock and my cancer would disappear. Neither proved to be true.

The rest was a hurried blur of IVs and questions. No, I wasn't allergic to any medicine (at least as far as I knew). *"Wasn't there a first time for everything?"* I thought.

My surgeon, Dr. Lee, appeared out of this hustle and bustle of personnel. *"How are you doing?"* he asked with a big grin on his face.

*"Fine, but that's not the question, Dr. Lee,"* I said. *"How are you doing?"*

*"I'm OK,"* he said.

*"That's not what I mean,"* I replied. *"Are you in the ZONE?"*

Poor bastard, I bet he was getting tired of hearing that from me, but I had to ask. He shook my hand.

*"Yes, Mr. Hill, I'm in the Zone,"* he said.

*"Then let's do this."*

Following Dr. Lee was the anesthesiologist who asked if I was ready for my "cocktail." I prayed this guy wasn't the reincarnation of Jim Jones. I'd seen *Guyana Tragedy* and it didn't have a happy ending.

I asked if there was a two-drink minimum and he assured me I wouldn't need more than one. He was right. The next thing I remember is waking up in the same room I'd started in. The only difference was that my stomach felt like I'd done about four thousand sit-ups and I was sure my bladder was about to explode.

Charlotte was there. Radiant. She took my hand in hers and said the only words I wanted to hear.

*"I talked with Dr. Lee,"* she said almost whispering. I couldn't tell if I was about to get good news or the "they tried" version of the story.

*"He says he can't be a hundred percent certain until the pathology report comes back,"* she continued, *"but, he says everything went well and he got it all. You're going to be fine."*

I smiled. She smiled. I drifted off to sleep.

Adios, Karl. I'll see you in my dreams.

———

If you're recently diagnosed, you probably picked up this book and blew past everything else just to get to this chapter.

I don't blame you. If this book had been around when I was diagnosed, I would have done the same thing. No offense taken. But promise me you'll at least skim the other parts. There's plenty of information here, and some sections will just make more sense to you at different stages of your journey.

Before I tell you what it's really like, it's important you understand my frame of reference so you can adjust your own expectations. I had a robotic-assisted laparoscopic radical prostatectomy (RLRP). At that time, I was forty-eight years old and in good health (*well, except for that little cancer problem*). This was my first surgery and only my second time being admitted to a hospital. I had no idea what to expect.

So what's prostate surgery really like? Here's the bumper sticker:

> Prostate Surgery
> It's not as painful as you think.
> Recovery takes longer than what
> you've been told.

Now that you've seen the headline, let's continue the story. I'll walk you through the day of your surgery.

Your surgery will probably be scheduled in the morning and they'll want you at the hospital around 6:00 a.m. The early start time isn't just because surgeons get up with the chickens (many do, but that's not why), it's because you'll have to fast at least twelve hours before the operation—no eating, no drinking, no nothing before the "Big Game." About the only thing you can do is brush your teeth. I did this as much for my surgeon as for myself!

When you get to the hospital, the front desk personnel will be cool, efficient, and hand you more paperwork. This is your first prostate operation, but it's just another day at the office for these folks. Most of the forms contain disclosure information the hospital is required to give you. It's all routine stuff. You won't remember any of it, but it does help pass the time before they call you back.

## All dressed up and no place to go

Once inside your hospital room, you'll be asked to undress and given a one-size-fits-all robe that doesn't. I've seen football players completely swallowed by these things. They're tents with arm holes. By the time you're dressed, you'll be met by a steady parade of more doctors and nurses with questions, and still more forms to complete. They'll want to make sure they're performing the right surgery on the right guy. You'll sign papers that give them the authority to open you up and ensure you're not allergic to any meds.

Soon, a nurse will get an IV started. You'll meet (briefly) with your anesthesiologist and he'll review his role. The surgeon will probably pay a visit. If you've given him specific instructions, as we discussed earlier, now is a good time to remind him of your requests. I had told my surgeon, "*When in doubt, cut it out!*" I repeated our "deal" and I felt better just saying it one last time.

A surgical nurse arrived and put a warm blanket on my legs. The next thing I remember is waking up in the room where it all began. The drugs are good. Correction—the drugs are *very* good. There's an amnesic quality to the anesthetic. You won't remember a single thing about the actual surgery.

It will take you a few hours to shake off the effects of the anesthesia. You'll slowly drag yourself back into consciousness and you'll probably do a system check of your body to gauge how you feel.

## How about pain?

How will you feel? Probably not as bad as you thought. My stomach felt as if I'd done thousands of sit-ups and my bladder was sending me signals that I really needed to pee. That was about it. You'll have a full complement of pain meds in your IV at this point, so speak up if you're experiencing any serious discomfort, and the doctors and nurses will help you through it. Some hospitals will ask you to rank your pain on a one to ten scale, with one being almost undetectable and ten being almost unbearable. They'll want you as close to a one as they can get.

The pain you *do* have—the "sit-up" pain—is due, of course, to the actual surgery. If you elect to have RLRP, there will be six surgical incisions in your abdomen—three small ones on the left side, two small ones on the right side, and about a two-inch incision just above your navel where the prostate is actually removed. If you choose the "open" traditional radical prostatectomy, you'll have a five- to six-inch incision just below your navel. You'll be stiff and sore, but able to move around in bed.

## What about the catheter?

The other discomfort you'll experience is the "full-bladder" feeling. I felt as if I had to urinate but couldn't; that's because the catheter was draining the urine from my body and collecting it in a bag.

The pain fades in a few hours when you finally come to grips with the fact that you don't have to get out of bed to relieve yourself. The good news is you get used to all of this in a relatively short time and you'll probably be comfortable with it before you're released from the hospital.

## Up and at 'em

If your surgery is in the morning, the nurses will likely have you out of bed by the early evening. You'll start with a few steps around your hospital room then progress to longer walks down the hospital hallway. The act of getting out of bed has as much of a psychological benefit as it does a physical effect. These are your first steps to recovery.

Your surgeon will make rounds the next morning and, in most cases, will release you if you had the laparoscopic procedure. Open procedure patients usually go home in about three days.

Whatever surgical procedure you chose, don't let your surgeon leave your room without getting a good idea of when you'll receive your pathology results. This is extremely important. Your pathology report is the definitive answer on the status of your cancer and whether it has spread beyond your prostate. Also, find out if the doctor's office will call you, or if you need to call them, to discuss the report.

## The Most Important Post-Op Questions to Ask Your Surgeon

1.  What did you take and why?

    Tip: Of course, he took your prostate; that's a no-brainer.

### What's the big idea?

The Amish believe every job is important, because everything—even the most routine task—glorifies God in some way. We could learn a lot from the Amish.

Even though you're worried and nervous, this is no time to be impatient or rude to anyone. These people are professionals who know the hospital drill better than you ever will. Treat them all with respect and courtesy, and you'll be repaid a hundred times over. They'll magically hear your buzzer when you call the nurse's station at 4:00 a.m. asking for a little more ice. Your IV will be administered with surprisingly little discomfort. Trust me. You just can't be too nice here.

What you're looking for here is if your surgeon had to take both sets of nerve bundles that control erection. Many surgeons today strive for a "nerve-sparing" radical prostatectomy whenever possible. Your chances for regaining full potency are improved if he was able to save one—or even better—both sets of nerves.

2. **Was the cancer contained in my prostate?**
Tip: If caught in the early stages before it spreads beyond the prostate capsule, the disease is almost 100 percent survivable.

3. **Can I get a copy of my pathology results?**
Tip: Of course, you can. In fact, your insurance carrier will probably insist on it and it's much easier to get a copy now than months after your surgery. Ask for it and get it.

4. **What are the chances of the cancer returning?**
Tip: This is the question you've wanted to ask all along, isn't it? Don't hesitate. Your surgeon will talk in percentages, but once he's seen your pathology report he can give you a good idea of what the future looks like.

The next important step you'll take is actually going home. Before you're released, they'll go over a complete set of post-op instructions. You'll receive prescriptions for an antibiotic, pain medications, and stool softeners, and, of course, your new best friend—a catheter.

Before you leave, you'll be told to arrange a follow-up appointment with your surgeon one week after surgery. During this office visit, the doctor will remove the catheter, examine your incisions, and check your overall progress.

## What you should remember at this point:
1. Treat all doctors, nurses, technicians—everyone associated with your care—with courtesy and it will pay dividends.
2. The pain is much less than what you imagine.

3. The catheter is a nuisance, but you'll get used to it fast.
4. Find out when you'll know the results of the pathology report and follow up to make sure you get a copy.

## Day 31, continued

I spent the next several hours fading in and out of a drug-induced sleep. When I was awake (rarely), the room spun like an out-of-control ride at an evil amusement park—kind of like Stephen King goes to Disneyland. It wasn't much fun.

I threw up on my favorite nurse and showered her with Sprite-scented puke. The anesthetic had made me nauseous and I was having a hard time coming out of it. A couple of new drugs to combat nausea had made me sleepy. I was having an impossible time staying awake. People came and went (mostly nurses who took more blood and kept a close watch on my vital signs) and a few friends. I waved drunkenly from the bed not really knowing who was standing in the doorway. I didn't really care.

## What's the big idea?

### Three Things No Doctor Will Tell You about Prostate Surgery

**1. It's not as painful as you think.**
You go to sleep. You wake up. It's over. Take the prescribed pain meds as long as you need them. The good news is you won't need them very long.

**2. Getting your bladder and bowels back to normal takes time.**
Don't let bloody urine throw you; you'll have it for a few days and it doesn't bother surgeons as much as you might think. As long as it's flowing and mixed with urine, your doctor will likely tell you not to worry about it (mine was a nice shade of "Hawaiian Punch" for almost two weeks!). Second, your first post-op bowel movement may be pretty uncomfortable. Consider drinking prune juice to get things started. Old age jokes aside, it really does work and the stuff doesn't taste nearly as bad as it sounds.

**3. Your penis will shrink.**
Sorry guys, it just does. With exercise (yes, there are exercises for the little general!) and time it will begin to resemble its former self, but it's going to be noticeably smaller.

A little after 1:00 a.m., my door opened and the night nurse came in. Perry Mason was on TV telling Della Street how he'd cracked the big case. Perry was in black and white and it suited him. I was in living color, but probably looked better in black and white. Perry looked good. I looked like shit.

*"Do you think you can stand for me?"* Audra the night nurse asked.

*"Yeah, I think so,"* I said probably a little too hesitantly.

*"OK, let's try,"* she said as she moved around to help me from the bed. This was going to be an adventure. I just knew it.

I let my left leg drop to the floor. It felt cold. I was glad I could feel it. The right leg was next. A little harder to move, but I let it drop the same way. Now both feet were on terra firma. Now the hard part.

I wiggled myself out of bed and used the IV stand to brace my stance. I wobbled a little and Audra reached out to grab me. We stood there, locked in a dancer's embrace, my right hand on her left shoulder, her right hand around my waist.

*"Audra,"* I croaked, my throat still dry from being intubated.

*"You're not going to fall are you? You can't fall. Dr. Lee will be all over me if I let you fall. Falling is a whole 'nother set of problems,"* she sputtered those words like the staccato repeat of an AK-47.

*"Audra,"* I continued, *"if we're going to dance, you'll have to lead. I'm just not up to any Fred and Ginger business."*

She laughed and one waltz around the tiny hospital room later I was back in bed.

Sleep came easily and the next few hours passed quickly. More vital signs were checked and doctors came and went. Dr. Lee came by to make his rounds. It was good to see him standing there, smiling—this guy who was about to start his day all over again by cutting up some other cancer patient. I was glad he was my doctor.

He repeated what he had told Charlotte. He couldn't be absolutely sure, he said, but he thought the pathology report would confirm what he believed to be true. He said he had gotten "IT" and everything looked good. Soon, I thought, Karl will be an unpleasant memory. Soon, I will be healed. Before that could happen, however, I had to be released from the hospital. Dr. Lee agreed and signed my discharge papers. I was going home.

Before I knew it, I was in the front seat of Charlotte's car heading home. The world sped by at 60 mph and it didn't appear to have changed. I was the one who was different. Those three and one-half hours on the operating table had changed my life forever. I wondered how different it would be as we made our way through the brown and gray tones of a Texas winter and found our way home.

———

# THE NEW & IMPROVED YOU

*Now with Less Prostate!*

# CHAPTER 7

# Coming home

You made it.

Your surgeon has released you from the hospital and now you're back home. The good news is you're past the surgery and can begin your recovery. The *bad* news is you have a long way to go.

How long?

It depends on the individual, the progress of the disease prior to surgery, and whether or not any follow up treatment is prescribed (e.g., chemotherapy). You'll be sent home with a complete list of instructions that cover wound and catheter care, acceptable activities, urinary control, sexual function, medications, and follow-up.

Here's a sneak peek at what you can expect.

## Wound care

You can begin showering immediately and you'll probably want

## What's the big idea?

Your first shower will be an experience. When you see yourself in the mirror for the very first time after surgery, you will look like you were in a knife fight—and lost. Imagine Frankenstein if Dr. F had been a more competent surgeon. Since the catheter is something you're probably not used to, I suggest getting in the shower before you disconnect the hose from the bag for the first time. Dealing with a catheter bag takes some practice; it's easy to slip or pull on the wrong end of the apparatus, and the result can be pretty messy. Do yourself a favor by starting out in the shower (without turning on the water). That way, if there is an accident, it's not a problem.

to. Your first shower will take a lot out of you, but you'll feel much better after cleaning up.

In most cases, your sutures will dissolve on their own. Each incision will be ringed with some redness but you'll be advised not to put antibiotic or other ointments on them.

## Catheter care

You'll be sent home with a catheter and it will remain in place anywhere from seven to fourteen days. How long depends on your doctor. Some guys have it removed in as little as five days; others have gone more than fifteen days. Be patient and don't push your doctor to remove it early. Remember, you were asleep when they inserted your catheter. If you have to have it reinserted because it was taken out too early, you'll be awake. Trust me on this one…asleep is better.

An overnight bag and a "leg" bag will be given to you. The larger overnight bag is aptly named; it holds plenty of fluid so you won't have to get up during the night to empty it. The smaller "leg" bag can be strapped to your calf for better mobility. Since it doesn't hold as much, this bag will have to be emptied regularly. It allows more movement, but you won't know when it has to be emptied, so you'll need to check it fairly often just to make sure.

# *Day 32*

The first thing I wanted to do was take a shower. I had to wash off the hospital smell as soon possible. The only problem was the tube coming from my penis and going into a catheter bag. Sure, we had gone to "catheter school" before they let us leave the hospital. This was something, after all, that would be a very important part of my life for the next week or so.

Charlotte turned on the water while I stood in the shower doorway waiting for it to warm up. She bent down to detach one end of the hose from the leg bag collecting my urine. I held the top of the hose to avoid any leakage.

She tugged. I tugged. Nothing moved.

Suddenly the hose came loose and I fumbled with my end of the connection. Charlotte was hit in the face with a flood of urine. It was like a *Three Stooges* routine where Moe was trying to figure out why water wouldn't come out of the hose and Curly turned on the faucet. SPLASH! Pee was everywhere. We brought Niagara Falls under control fast. But, fast is a relative term when you're being pissed on. Fast is never fast enough when you're getting a face full of urine.

*"That went well,"* I said.

*"Live and learn,"* Charlotte added as she wiped her urine-soaked face and clothes.

*"I think I'll get in the shower now,"* I said. "I can take it from here."

Charlotte didn't argue. A face full of pee will do that to a person.

---

## Activities

You won't be able to drive for at least a week (don't even think of driving with a catheter!). Once the catheter is removed, you can get back behind the wheel so long as you're off prescription pain medication.

Vigorous activities (jogging, golf, and exercising) are off-limits for at least six weeks after your surgery. After six weeks, your doctor will likely allow you to resume normal activities.

## Urinary control

You won't have any at first. As long as the catheter is in place, it will take care of that for you. Once it's removed, you will slowly regain control of your bladder—some guys are fully continent from day one, others take longer. We'll cover this in more detail a little further in this chapter.

## Sexual function

Some doctors prescribe Viagra® or other erectile dysfunction medications immediately after surgery to stimulate blood flow to the penis. I know guys who have actually regained partial erections with the catheter still in place. This is rare. A lot depends on whether or not your physician was able to save one or both sets of nerves that control erections.

As a rule of thumb, it can take anywhere from six to eighteen months of recovery before you can achieve an erection suitable for intercourse. In some men, it can take even longer. The good news here is that you don't need an erection to experience an orgasm, something we'll cover in detail in chapter 10.

## Medications

You'll come home with prescriptions for a high-powered antibiotic, a pain-killer, and a stool softener. They'll also suggest drinking prune juice or using an over-the-counter medication to help you resume regularity.

## Follow-up

Assuming everything goes according to plan, your first follow-up visit will be one week after your surgery. During this appointment, you'll get a complete checkup to see how you're healing and they'll remove your catheter.

## The five things you must have when you get home:

The first couple of days after surgery will pass in a blur. Credit the pain meds or the aftereffects of the anesthesia, but, trust me, you won't remember much. You'll sleep a lot, partially because you're weak from the surgery and probably because you're just relieved it's over.

The medication should do a good job of knocking out any pain you're feeling. Soon, you'll be off the hard stuff and back to over-the-counter medications like Tylenol or Advil. It really depends on the type of surgery you had. Doctors will tell you patients who take the laparoscopic route usually have less pain than those who choose the traditional "open" radical prostatectomy. I think a lot has to do with the patient. We all know guys who could probably do this wide awake while chewing on a piece of beef jerky. Other guys faint at the first sign of the needle. My own experience was somewhere in between.

During this first week at home, while you're anxiously waiting to ditch your new best friend (your catheter), you'll need a few special things to keep you comfortable. Here are the five things I think every recovering prostate surgery patient should have at home:

1. **A great gadget**

   TiVo is a great gadget. It's a DVR (digital video recorder) that can hold eighty plus hours of movies, television shows, documentaries, and anything else that's broadcast into your home. TiVo is great for the recovering prostate patient because you never have to get out of bed to change the DVD. Think about it; eighty hours is over three full days of programming. That's a lot of TV!

2. **Good food**

   Your doctor will probably hate me for saying this, but now that you're home, it's time to screw the diet. You likely dropped a few pounds in the hospital anyway and some comfort food may be just the ticket to improving your mental and physical well-being. Like ice cream? Eat your favorite flavor and then take a nap watching something you recorded on TiVo.

3. **Comfortable clothes**

   You just had major surgery, so naturally you are sore. Boxer shorts work great with a catheter. The hose won't get tangled up and they're easy to put on and take off. You'll also need some soft, loose-fitting shirts. Your abdomen is going to be tender for a few weeks while your sutures heal and you don't want anything chafing you.

4. **Coccyx cushion**

   You've seen these things before—people call them "donuts" or "chair rings." They all provide the same function; they take pressure off your coccyx (your tailbone). There are several varieties—some are foam-filled, others are inflatable. Whatever you choose, you're going to need one. Your coccyx will be sore for weeks after your surgery. Don't even *think* of sitting in a hard chair without one.

5. **A leg up**

You're going to need some help getting in and out of bed. If your bed sits high off the floor, I suggest using a small, sturdy step stool to assist you. If you take that route, get an aluminum one that has handrails on the sides so you can brace yourself. I know guys who didn't recuperate in bed at all; they chose their favorite recliner. A recliner works great if that's what you like.

You'll be spending a lot of time flat on your back during those first few days of recovery. Yes, walking will be part of your daily routine, but just going from one side of your place to the other will tire you at first. It takes time to regain your strength, and bed rest is part of the healing process.

## Making your recuperation the best it can be

Anything that takes your mind off things can be a blessing during this phase of your recovery. You'll find yourself doing a lot of waiting during this time period—waiting for the results of your pathology report, waiting to have your catheter removed, waiting for your strength to return. The time will go a whole lot faster if you have something to occupy your mind. Here are some suggestions.

- **Movies and all of their sequels**

Any movie with a sequel will do. If you like action films, Bruce Willis' *Die Hard* series is good. There are dozens of comedies with follow-ups, from *Airplane!* to *Scary Movie* to the *National Lampoon Vacation* films. They're all great for a laugh. Thanks to my wife, I rediscovered the *Godfather* trilogy. I'd seen the first *Godfather* movie, but had never gotten around to *Godfather II* and *III*. These are excellent choices (OK, with the possible exception of Sofia Coppola's performance in *Godfather III*), and when they're seen in rapid succession you can really get caught up in the story. My all-time favorite series is Steven Spielberg's *Band of Brothers*. This incredible saga of courage captivated me for several days. I was (almost) sorry to see World War II end.

- **Music**

  If you're a music lover, I strongly encourage you to get an iPod or some other MP3 player. The best thing about the iPod and its digital cousins is that once they're loaded with your favorite songs you never have to change out a CD. The batteries also last a long time before they need recharging. There are also some great options for free online music. My favorite is Pandora (www.pandora.com). This online music site lets you select up to 100 artists for your personal playlist and the music is non-stop.

- **Books on CD**

  The public library can be a treasure trove of free entertainment. I suggest taking a trip to your local library and checking out some of your favorite authors. The CD books will usually range from eleven to sixteen compact disks, and this is a great way to either entertain yourself or lull you to sleep.

- **Friends**

  Your friends will want to know how you're doing. Once your strength starts returning, see visitors as much as you are comfortable. News from the outside world can help brighten your day and some encouraging words are always welcome.

- **Phone calls**

  We live in a world with one ear glued to a cell phone. Keep one beside you so you won't have to get out of bed to have contact with the outside world.

# *Day 38*

Dr. Lee returned our call. Since we hadn't spoken with him directly since my surgery, it was good to hear his voice. I asked the question I'd wanted answered since the day Dr. Price told me I had cancer.

*"Have you gotten the pathology report back?"* I asked maybe a little too tentatively.

*"Yes, we got it the other day,"* he said.

*"Well…"* I replied. Would this be the good news? Or would I be sent hurly-burly into the fire—have to find a good oncologist and start this process over again. Was this road coming to an end, or had we reached the crossroads? I couldn't wait for his answer.

*"We got it all. It looks good. You're clear of cancer,"* he said with the same nonchalant tone that Dr. Price had given me the "bad" news. These guys were pros in the news delivery business. *"Never let 'em see you sweat,"* seemed to be their mantra. Good news, like bad news all came at…the…same… measured…pace.

I clutched the phone to my chest as tears filled my eyes. Charlotte was on the extension. She screamed with joy. We laughed. We thanked God. We thanked Dr. Lee. We thanked each other. We thanked and thanked until we ran out of breath. Dr. Lee, always the passive observer, heard this melee over the phone and let us savor the moment.

Everybody needs a little good news from time to time. It was finally our turn. I was grateful. I was happy that the outlook for me had improved. I could handle the rest of this stuff because I finally knew the truth—

Dr. Lee had killed Karl and he was out of my life.

———

## It's in the bag: Your brief life with a catheter

Throughout the first week or so of recovery, you'll be tethered to a catheter. It's not like you have an option; all recovering prostate surgery patients go home with one. The catheter is there to drain urine from your body while your urethra heals from the procedure.

Having a catheter sounds much worse than it actually is. You may be a little embarrassed to carry around a bag filled with your urine, but you'll get used to it in a surprisingly short time.

Of course, the good news is that you won't need a catheter very long. Most doctors remove them within a week or two after surgery. Since you've probably never had a catheter before, here are some tips that will help.

- **Boxers or briefs?**
  *Definitely* boxers. Purchase some loose-fitting boxer shorts before your surgery and wear them as a substitute for pants while the catheter is in place. It will make it easier to empty the catheter bag and the wide leg holes allow plenty of room for the catheter tube.

- **Go with the flow**
  When it comes to catheters, gravity is your best friend. Always make sure your catheter bag is positioned below your penis so the urine flows *away* from your body. Also make sure there are never any kinks or knots in the tube to keep the urine from backing up. You never want the urine to flow back toward you. You'll get a rude shock the first time this happens. The backwash will deliver a feeling like having white-hot needles inserted into your penis. It's not any fun.

- **A little dab'll do you**
  Put small amount of antibiotic ointment around the catheter tube at the tip of your penis once or twice a day. This will make you more comfortable and help protect against infection.

## What's the big idea?

Keep your overnight catheter bag in a mop bucket beside your bed just in case the hose isn't secured firmly to the bag. If there's a leak in the middle of the night, it won't be a problem when you wake up.

## Removing the catheter

In seven to fourteen days, you'll have your first follow-up visit with your surgeon. It's during this appointment that—if everything is going according to plan—you'll say good-bye to the catheter. It's a happy day for most guys.

Getting the catheter removed isn't nearly as unpleasant as you might think. The whole procedure takes under a minute. You'll be standing and the nurse will insert an empty syringe into the "Y" of the rubber catheter hose. The nurse will draw out the saline solution from the small balloon that's holding the catheter in place in your bladder. Once this balloon deflates, she or he will gently pull on the catheter hose and it will slide out of your body.

Once the hose comes out, you'll probably pee all over the floor. Don't be embarrassed. It's natural. They expect it. As my doctor's nurse said to me, *"That's why we have tile instead of carpet!"* No big deal.

Wear an adult incontinence pad the day your catheter is removed. You may need it; you may not, but it will make the ride home a lot more pleasant.

# *Day 43*

I noticed my urine was still a lovely shade of "Hawaiian Punch" (something from the berry family of flavors) as I looked at the small drops that leaked from me in the shower. I was ready to free myself from this tether connected to my penis. Beyond the fact that it was wholly uncomfortable, it was a constant reminder that yes, I was sick, very sick. I wanted the reminder out of me.

Dr. Lee took a quick look at my incisions—six in total: five "small" ones (three on the left side of my navel, two on the right) and one approximately five-inch-long incision where he removed my prostate. I'd always heard the prostate was a "walnut-sized" gland. Judging by the incision, however, my prostate must have been about the size of a plum tomato. I was happy to have the cancerous tomato removed from my body, even if it meant a scar that reminded me of Herman Munster.

After the brief exam, Dr. Lee said I was making excellent progress. He scheduled a follow-up appointment in ninety days to check my PSA. I didn't know if he was tired of seeing so much of me or if I was really improving. It didn't matter much. I was anxious to move on.

"*Are you ready to have your catheter out?*" the nurse said when she entered the room after Dr. Lee's departure.

Charlotte looked at the nurse and turned pale. "*We're close, but I think I'll pass on seeing this,*" she said as she backed her way out of the exam room.

"*Can't say I blame you,*" I said. If I could have gone with her and had someone describe it to me, I would have gladly followed her to the waiting room.

"*Ready?*" the nurse asked again.

"*Yes,*" I said.

"*Drop your pants and we'll get moving,*" she instructed as she unwrapped a sterile syringe from a plastic bag.

She asked me to disconnect the catheter from my leg bag. The "Hawaiian Punch" pouch of urine clung to my calf like a parasite. All I could think was that the "moment" had finally arrived.

"*Deep breath,*" she ordered as she drew the saline from the bag inside my bladder. I could feel something happening deep inside me. It felt as if something had crawled up my penis and now was looking for a way out. I held my breath as instructed.

"*Here we go,*" she said.

Zipppppppppp was the sound the tube made as she tugged on it, pulling it out of my penis.

"*I….*" was all I could say as I exhaled.

Then I peed Hawaiian Punch all over the exam room floor. The steady stream of very-berry urine just wouldn't stop.

*"I'm so sorry,"* I said standing there with my pants around my ankles and a nurse staring at my penis. *"I just can't seem to—"* I continued before she stopped me.

*"No big deal,"* she said. *"Now you know why there's no carpet in here."* She laughed.

*"Is that it?"* I asked.

*"You're done,"* she said.

*"Thanks,"* I said. *"You did a great job. Sorry about the floor."*

*"Happens all the time,"* she replied. *"We're pretty used to it."*

That made *one* of us.

My penis hurt, but not as much as I feared. I shuffled like an old man to the patient pickup in front of the hospital. I was finally going home. A home without a tube in my penis and a bag strapped to my leg.

Progress.

Finally.

———

## Dealing with incontinence

Some guys are fully continent the minute the catheter is removed. Most aren't. Regardless of your experience, remember that your body has just been through a traumatic event and it just takes time to heal.

A lot depends on your age, stage, and general health before surgery. It took me about six months before I was fully continent. Some guys take less time; some guys take more.

You'll need some adult protection until you're fully continent. Here's what I used:

### *Depends Guards for Men*

These work very well. They're easy to use and they hold plenty of fluid. You'll probably go through several daily during the early phase of your recovery. They won't let you down, but you'll be a lot more comfortable if you change them often. Since they hold a lot of fluid, you might want to try to save a few bucks by changing them only when you absolutely have to. Don't. You'll be a lot happier if you replace them when they begin to feel heavy.

## Adult diapers

I know, it sounds gross but they work very well at night. Think of these as you would your "nighttime" catheter bag. You wear them just like briefs and you won't have to worry about making a mess if your body doesn't send you a signal to get up and pee in the middle of the night.

## Thin panty liners

Another thing that sounds unpleasant, but you'll actually be happy when you progress to this stage. Thin liners are a lot more comfortable than guards and diapers and they'll give you the protection you'll need during the final stages of your return to full continence.

# Day 44 to 46

In years past, Charlotte and I enjoyed the day after Christmas; we'd hit the after-Christmas sales and spend the day jostling with the crowds. It was always a little frenetic, but a lot of fun. Not this year. I spent the day watching *Lawrence of Arabia* on DVD and resting up from all of the family visits Christmas day. I hated to admit it, but all of that activity was tiring. I don't know what was worse, trying to act as if I was OK, or just pulling myself through it. It didn't matter, because it was over and I was glad to be past massive doses of concerned family for the immediate future.

## What's the big idea?

Measure your progress in weeks and months, not days, and you'll be a lot happier.

You'll hear this often: *"It just takes time."* They're right. It *does* take time for your body to heal. But regardless of how long it takes, it's probably going to be too long for your patience.

Give yourself a break on this one. Do your exercises as your physician directs, but then let your body work its healing magic. You'll look back in a few months and be amazed at how far you've come.

Back to recovery…

This is something that's demanded my complete attention. My continence…er, rather *incontinence*…has become a real issue. When I stand, I'm afraid I'll literally wet my pants. When I walk, it's an exercise in clinching my sphincter muscle while moving my feet forward. It's like learning to walk while learning not to pee all over again.

If I were even 50 percent continent, I would feel as if I could take on the world. If I were honest and rated myself according to the "pain scale" used in the hospital, I would say my pain is a one or two. My continence, with one being no control at all and ten being absolute control, would be around two also. If I sit in the same place and don't move, I have a modest amount of control. The moment I get up to relieve myself, my body starts without me. It doesn't seem to remember that it needs to wait until I make it to the bathroom. My bladder has a mind of its own. It would be good someday for it to remember its manners. I guess I'll just have to continue exercising and waiting for that day to come.

If patience is a virtue, I'm not very virtuous. I want to recover. I want to improve—at least one step a day, each twenty-four-hour period better than the last.

I want my old pre-prostate-cancer life back.

NOW.

———

## A word about Kegel exercises

By now, you've been advised to do Kegel exercises to strengthen your urinary muscles. Kegel exercises help build up the pelvic muscles so you can regain continence. You can identify and isolate these muscles by starting and stopping the flow of urine. Once you've located the muscles, simply tighten and relax them as a part of your exercise routine.

Kegels are extremely important to helping you reclaim continence. What doctors *won't* tell you, however, is that you shouldn't *overdo* them.

Some guys think doing Kegels several times a day can speed up the recovery process when the opposite is true. Too much and your body can become overtired, leaving you with less control than before you exercised. Take it easy at first and don't overdo it.

When I began my Kegels, I was doing one set of ten (tightening the muscle for a count of ten; releasing it for a count of ten; ten times in a row) every hour. That was way over the top! I developed muscular spasms and caused myself a lot of pain. When I finally told my surgeon about this, he directed me to do the exercises as described twice daily, not the eight times a day I had been doing. The spasms went away and slowly, but surely, I regained full continence.

# Day 47–48

I peed when I sat down. I peed when I stood up. I peed when I reclined. I peed when I bent over. I peed when I sneezed and I peed when I coughed.

I peed.

My urine was steadily progressing from Hawaiian Punch to amber. Progress. At least, I was moving away from blood loss and more toward a "normal" color. Any way you look at it, there's something disquieting about blood pouring out of your body, no matter what orifice it chooses. It made me a little sick to my stomach.

I watched the entire *Band of Brothers* DVD collection. Steven Spielberg and Tom Hanks captured the history of 101st Airborne's "Easy Company" in a masterful bit of storytelling. I was entranced for days. I watched this for entertainment value and it took my mind off my recovery. Seeing the men fighting their way out of the Battle of the Bulge made my problems seem small. They were dying for freedom. All I was fighting for was to regain control of my bladder. If they could defeat the Nazis, I could whip my bladder into shape. As it turned out, both would be a lot harder than either of us imagined.

———

## Walk it off

Once your catheter is removed, it'll be a lot easier to get around. Even with a pad or liner, you'll find that walking is a great way to regain your strength. Start out with small goals such as walking to and from the refrigerator a few times each day and progress to walks outside your home or apartment. Get comfortable with one distance before tackling another. Think of your recovery like a marathon, not a sprint; you have to build up your strength so you can go the distance.

It's great if you have a companion to walk with, but if you don't, make sure you take a cell phone just in case you get into trouble. The important thing to remember is that exercise is a must, but as with Kegel exercises, you'll regret it if you overdo. Set goals and achieve them, but don't push your body too hard. You won't like it when it pushes back.

# *Day 53*

Linda Storer called late in the day to check in on me. Linda is the only other cancer survivor (breast: double mastectomy) that I know. Linda and I have a developed a sort of "disease bond" that cancer survivors share. We both beat our personal Karls and lived to tell about it.

*"Have you been depressed?"* Linda asked.

*"A little,"* I answered, surprised at my truthfulness. *"I guess it's natural."*

*"I was depressed for a while, too. It goes away though. It doesn't last forever,"* she replied. *"What are you depressed about?"*

*"I dunno, I guess how slow my recovery is going,"* I said. *"I know it's only been two weeks since I got my catheter removed, but it's not any fun trying to retrain your body. If you know what I mean."*

She did.

*"I'm also paranoid about any little aches and pains. I'm so dialed into my body that it's making me a little nuts,"* I continued.

*"I know what you mean,"* she said. *"For the longest time, I thought my cancer was coming back each time I felt something. That passes with time too."*

"OK," I said. "Here's a question for you. How long before you quit looking over your shoulder?" I asked.

"For me, it took a couple of years," she answered. "Getting diagnosed with cancer is something I don't think you ever really get over. You just learn to live with it."

"I don't think I'll ever forget my diagnosis or hearing the words 'you've got cancer,' for as long as I live," I added. "It's something that sticks with you. It's not every day you get a death sentence."

"I know what you mean, but I'm here to tell you it does get better. You'll be amazed at how time can heal a lot of this. Your wounds will heal. The scars—inside and out—will fade," she said.

I told Charlotte about my conversation with Linda later in the day.

Charlotte is convinced that her phone call is another example of God sending angels to help us. Maybe she's right. The call did come at a time when there was no one else in the house. I was the only one who could answer the phone and unlike so many times before, I felt oddly compelled to answer the call. I made a real effort to do it, something I haven't done throughout my recuperation.

Angels among us?

It doesn't matter where you are in your spiritual journey; the thought of God caring enough to have someone reach out to you means something.

---

## Your mileage may vary: Keeping your expectations in check

One of the most difficult aspects of recovering from prostate surgery is managing your expectations. For example, I was really down when

## What's the big idea?

Cancer robs you of so many things. Once you get it, you may find it difficult to relax completely. Resist the urge to constantly look over your shoulder and wonder what that pain *really* is. Don't waste time wondering if the clock is ticking on your time, or even worse, trying to calculate how much time you have *left*. Give yourself a break and celebrate the countless victories of your recovery—no matter how small. It might just be a day with one fewer incontinence pad, but it's progress and it's worth celebrating.

I wasn't fully continent within a couple of days of having my catheter removed. I'd read about guys who walked out of their doctor's offices fully continent. That wasn't me, and it really depressed me.

When I finally learned to measure my progress in weeks and months—not hours and days—I became a much happier person. I can't stress enough that *your mileage may vary.* Just because you've read about someone else experiencing a rapid recovery, that doesn't necessarily mean it will happen to you. It doesn't mean it won't either, but you have to be prepared for the long haul. We may live in the land of the microwave oven but some things aren't ready in a minute. Be patient with yourself and you'll be a lot happier.

# *Day 60*

Today is my anniversary.

Exactly one month ago, I had robotic LRP. I can honestly say I feel one hell of a lot better today than I did one month ago.

Historical perspective can improve your outlook on your current situation. It's kind of like standing at the back of a long line—you always feel better when another guy gets in line behind you. Suddenly, you're not at the end anymore.

That's how it is with prostate cancer surgery. Each day beyond your surgery, you feel like you're moving up in the line. You may not be able to see it, but you are advancing. Sadly, the disease keeps putting guys in line behind you. By the time you're recovered, you can look over your shoulder and see it snaking out the door, down the block, and around the corner… and around the world. The line never ends because there are always more guys queuing up for their turn.

How have I improved in one month?

- Back at the office for four to five hours each day (I could go a little longer, but my wife and business partner won't hear of it!)
- Walking one mile each day

- Climbing the stairs (all nineteen of 'em) in our two-story home
- Pretty much pain free (I take Advil at night, mainly out of habit)
- Continent (er…well, not yet but I'm working on it); I use anywhere from two to three Depends Guards for Men each day, but it's getting better slowly.
- THE BEST PART? I AM CANCER FREE!

Things *ARE* getting better. I'm hoping I can look back on this page one month from today and marvel at the progress I've made. I want to be able to say, *"Wow! What was he so worried about?"* I'll let you know in a month.

———

## What you should remember at this point:

1. Follow your post-op instructions.
2. Accept help from family, friends, and co-workers.
3. Measure your progress in weeks and months, not days.
4. Exercise, but don't OVER exercise; too much can actually slow your recovery.
5. Be good to yourself; stock up on comfort foods and plenty of things to entertain you while you recover.

# CHAPTER 8

# Four things every woman should know about prostate cancer

## *Day 63*

Charlotte and I were intimate tonight for the first time since my surgery. It was low-impact relations due to my slowly improving condition, but it was very satisfying for both of us. It gave me hope of a day in the future when I'll be more of a full-scale partner. It felt good to be close. It felt even better just to *feel*. I was grateful for the experience and touched by her willingness—eagerness—to take the first tentative steps to rekindle this part of our relationship.

I'm retraining myself in so many areas I used to take for granted—continence, sexual performance. It's depressing. Charlotte is learning what it's like to live with someone going through this experience, all the while teaching herself the "new" rules of intimacy for both of us. It's a class neither of us signed up for, but we're taking it. I believe we'll become good students before we reach graduation day.

———

The day after my diagnosis my wife summed up prostate cancer well: *"It's about the worst disease a man can get."*

I corrected her without missing a beat.

*"No,"* I said. *"It's not about the worst disease a man can get. It is the worst disease a man can get."*

She had no idea.

I knew the morning of my diagnosis that my life—our life—was in for a huge change. This was big...ATOM BOMB big. The life I had known when I walked into that exam room was officially over. I was now the guy with <u>cancer</u>. Worst of all, I didn't know where to turn or what to do next. By the time we walked out of the doctor's office, I was a zombie. I fell back on the only thing that even came close to making me feel like a man. I held my wife in an empty elevator and told her everything was going to be "OK." The truth is, I'd never felt so alone in my life. I didn't have a clue.

My wife was desperate and determined to help me. At first, I was just as desperate and determined *not* to let her help. I could handle this all by myself. It was as if I had stepped fully formed out of a celluloid frame from a John Ford western.

If you haven't figured it out yet, men are different. This goes a lot deeper than what you learned in fifth grade health class. We think differently. We react differently. And we deal with difficult situations differently.

When we received the cancer diagnosis, my wife became emotional.

I became angry.

She became supportive.

I became defensive.

See the difference?

I actually said these words to her in the car on our way back from the doctor: *"Don't feel sorry for me. I don't feel sorry for myself."* To this day, I have no idea what made me say that. Up until then, I was a normal, rational, healthy middle-aged male. Three words in a doctor's office had turned me into a middle-aged *asshole*.

Hey, gimme a break. I had cancer.

Contrary to what you may think at this point in your relationship, guys really aren't hopeless. If someone you love has been diagnosed with prostate cancer, don't give up. With knowledge and understanding, you can help him beat the disease and build an even stronger relationship.

Here are the four things every woman should know about men and prostate cancer.

1. **He'll go through every stage of grief in no particular order.**

   If you go with your husband to get the results of his biopsy *(no matter what he tells you—GO!)*, there's something you need to know. There's a very good chance he's already done a little prostate cancer homework. That means he's probably already moving past the first stage of grief: denial. He's rounding the corner and coming up on stage two: anger.

   He's not jumping the gun. Your husband is sliding into anger because he's already endured a transrectal ultrasound and biopsy. It's an unpleasant procedure (think thirty-minute Pap test with a lot more pain) and he waddled out of that exam room in search of some answers. He found just enough information to make him dangerous and he hasn't told you what he suspects. Why? He didn't want you to worry. He didn't want you think he was less of a man. He didn't want you to feel sorry for him. All perfectly good reasons, if you're a guy.

   What can you do to help? Join his team. Begin by helping him find answers to his questions. He just thought he was prepared when he walked into that exam room. He wasn't. Nobody is.

   He has a million questions racing through his head and he's hungry for answers. Go with him to the bookstore, the library, or online. Ask your friends if they know anyone else experiencing prostate cancer and talk with them. Help him turn his "noes" into "knows." It's you and him against this disease. Become a team and help him turn his anger into a hunger—for answers. Your goal is to help make him the best-informed prostate cancer patient possible.

   With all of this information, will he still be angry? Maybe. But, the more he learns, the more likely he will be to let go of some of his resentment. It's true what they say: *knowledge is power*. The information is likely to give him a new sense of power—of regaining control over his own destiny.

   You'll be less afraid too. And you'll both be in a much better position to make the right decisions on treatment and have a clearer idea of what to expect.

2. **He'll fight the disease and maybe you along with it.**

   Get ready. You're in for a few arguments. Men and women really *don't* see things the same way. My first instinct was to adopt a "me-against-the-world" attitude. It didn't do either of us any good. My wife helped me overcome this by nurturing a "team" spirit. After a while, we became a dedicated force ready to navigate our way through the prostate cancer maze.

That's not to say that your guy will always be open to your ideas or suggestions. He won't. Give him a little room. If you meet resistance, try again later. Allow him to get used to each new situation before he's forced to accept something else. Let him negotiate the pace and guide him toward the best treatment, care, doctors, and advice.

Men aren't stupid. They really do know they can't negotiate their way out of prostate cancer. Many believe, however, they may be able to cut a deal with the available treatments so they'll come out with at least something resembling their current life.

When I was diagnosed, I had already done some homework. I was rounding the corner of grief stage three, bargaining, when I walked into my physician's office. Due to my age and cancer stage, Urology Associates of North Texas doctor Gary Price immediately recommended surgery.

I had a counteroffer. *"How about seeds?"* I said. "Seeds" is a common term for radioactive grain-of-rice-sized pellets used to treat prostate cancer in some men. Dr. Price was quick to call my hand.

*"No,"* he said, *"seeds aren't right for you."*

I lost round one of negotiation. I hoped I would have better luck with the others.

It's not easy for any guy to come to terms with prostate cancer. It takes some getting used to. My wife didn't rush it. After the decision was made for surgery and the date was set, she carefully helped me prepare for my postoperative life. First, she coaxed me into shopping with her for comfortable clothes to wear during recovery. Then she encouraged me to get out with my friends as much as possible prior to the BIG DAY. We read books on the disease and talked about what we found. We searched for answers and discovered that we became a little less afraid the more we talked about it. We were a dedicated force ready to navigate and negotiate our way through the prostate cancer maze.

Understand, of course, that your guy won't always be open to your ideas or suggestions. Give him space and time. If he resists your ideas, don't push; fall back and try it again later. Most men will feel more than a little overwhelmed with all of the life-changing decisions they're suddenly forced to make. It's hard going through this, but it's even harder for your guy to see the people he loves go through this with him.

Guys won't admit to being self-conscious, but many are. It's likely that he suddenly feels everyone is looking at him differently, and that makes him uncomfortable. You can help by suggesting he take things a step at a time. Encourage him to pause long enough to get used to each new situation before trying to accept something else that's new.

Celebrate small victories like choosing the treatment, finding a doctor you both trust, and coming home from the hospital. Let him negotiate the pace, but be positive and do your best to help him find the good in the obstacle course he is facing.

3. **He'll be depressed. OK, make that *really* depressed.**

Depression is a BIG issue with cancer patients. A good friend of mine once described cancer as a religious train wreck—kind of like my karma ran over your dogma. He said that, even though he was terminal, he was *lucky*. I couldn't understand why he felt so fortunate.

*"We're all going to die,"* he said. *"I'm lucky because I know <u>when</u>."* For a guy with a few months to live, he had an amazingly upbeat attitude.

Your man will encounter depression. This is normal. Deep depression—anything more than a "case of the blues" that lasts longer than two weeks—deserves fast medical attention. This isn't something to negotiate. If you suspect your guy is suicidal, get professional help immediately.

# *Day 64*

What will the New Year bring for me and my family? Based on my recent experience, I can only say one thing: *"Who knows?"*

If you had predicted the events of the past year to me on January 1, I would have said you were crazy. I do believe that bad things happen to good people. I also believe that good things happen to bad people. I basically believe that things just happen. Some guys win the lottery and others get killed by a falling piano. Shit happens. Sometimes it happens to you.

What have I learned in the past year? That's a book by itself. I have, however, reexamined what I believe to be important. The list:

- Health
- Faith
- Family
- Friends

OK, I know there's no real "new" or innovative information in that list. What *is* new is how I *perceive* it.

Here's how this works.

You really *don't* miss your health until it's up for grabs. You really *don't* consider your faith until it's the only thing standing between you and the eternal abyss. You *don't* think about your family until they're the last hands you hold before you cross into something terrifyingly uncertain. You *don't* fully appreciate your friends until you realize they're the only thing giving your family comfort when you can't. It really does give you a different perspective on the world and how you live in it. Trust me; it matters.

I am sure God is tired of hearing this by now, but each day I pray the same prayer. I pray for my family and friends. I pray for my glacier-slow recovery. I don't ask for miracles. No. I humbly ask for progress—this day a little less pain than the day before, this day a little more strength, this day a little continence, this day a little better than the day before.

One more step down the path.

When will I reach the finish line? I don't know. I say I don't pray for miracles, but there is some small part of me that does. I'm like a three-year-old with no concept of time. I wake up each morning and wonder, *"Is today Christmas?"*

In my adult world, it's a little different. Each day I wake up and say to myself, "Is this the day it doesn't hurt anymore? Is this the day when I can go from four incontinence pads to three to two? Is this THE DAY?

Is today Christmas? No, it's New Year's Day, a day when we wipe the slate clean and start over. It's like the opening day of baseball season where every team is in first place; everybody bats 350 and has a shot at the All-Star Game.

Can I take the pennant this year? I don't really care. I'm just looking to finish the season with more wins than losses. I want what I pray for: each day a little better than the last. One more step forward.

———

Some men are depressed immediately after diagnosis. It doesn't hit others until they begin recovery and encounter one of the more feared byproducts of treatment, like erectile dysfunction (ED, also known as impotence). It's a frightening thought—the prospect of losing your "manhood"—even if only temporarily.

ED is a common side effect of prostate cancer surgery. In some men, it lasts for a brief time. In others, it lingers for weeks, months, even years. My surgeon told me that it could take eighteen to thirty-six months after surgery to regain an erection. You read right—a year and a half to three years. That's a long time for anyone. It's an eternity for a type-A personality! Was I depressed? Yes! But, I was also blessed with a spouse who understood what I was fighting as a man and what we were facing as a couple.

The fear and depression faded in time. I was lucky. Even though I encountered the dreaded "ED," I had a spouse who wanted to move forward instead of looking back. And, together, we learned a new dance.

It may sound like a cliché, but nobody can tell you what it feels like to be diagnosed with cancer. What you can know, however, is that—regardless of the outcome—it changes people for the rest of their lives. You look at life with a different perspective. Some things that were terribly important before diagnosis don't seem like such a big deal after. For some men, this can impact their work performance or the way they interact with others. A guy that jumped out of bed every morning to get to the office may linger a little longer in the shower.

I spent almost an entire year trying to regain my sense of drive and direction. I found that even though I wasn't terminal, I just didn't have the usual patience for some people, places, or things. It takes time to get past this point. As recovery progresses, so does the attitude. Be patient. If you think you know 100 percent of what your spouse is going through, you're fooling yourself. You probably know only about 10 percent. Your guy is an iceberg. There's a lot below the surface you'll never see.

# *Day 84*

Another long day.

It's happening. I am being sucked back into the workaday world I left so ungraciously almost two months ago. Lying in a hospital bed with an IV in my arm, I told myself I would be different when I got out.

Turns out, I *am* different.

I *don't have a prostate.*

I *don't have complete control of my bladder.*

I *don't have erections.*

I (this is the only good part) ***don't* have cancer.**

Sure, it sounds appealing, but it is depressing as hell. I'm basically the same guy, just wetter and less fun.

Here's why I feel this way. Today, I worked another ten-hour day. It was fire-drill filled with deadlines, budgets, and the usual stuff. As I sorted through it all, I had a nagging sense that it just didn't add up to much. To be fair, nothing really looks big compared to cancer.

What have I been saying? Oh yeah, *"I want my old life back."* Well, sort of. Continence *would* be nice, and the ability to have an erection would be *terrific.* These things, they tell me, can return in time. I hope so.

How about my sense of purpose? When will it return? Dodging the cancer bullet (if I really have dodged it) *should mean* something. My body knows I've been through a life-changing event—maybe it's time I convinced my mind.

When you work a ten-hour day, you leave everyone with the impression that "you're back."

Here's the question for today: *How do you convince yourself?*

———

4.  **He'll heal faster with an attitude of gratitude.**

    Acceptance is the final stage of grief for a very good reason. If you've made it through the first four stages—denial, anger, bargaining, and depression—you either accept things for what they are, or you call the front desk and check out early. I chose to accept things the way they were.

    My wife helped a lot. How? First, she accepted me for what I had become. She embraced every stage of my recovery and provided me the moral support necessary to move beyond whatever roadblock I was facing. Time, at least to her, was the cherished commodity. Nothing else mattered. The important thing was that we had the time *together.* As far as she was concerned, we could overcome difficulties like impotence and incontinence. The important thing to her was that we had received a second chance. We had been given the time to work out the other things and they would be resolved on their own schedule.

    Her unconditional acceptance helped me develop an attitude of gratitude. Most people are harder on themselves than they are on others. I was no exception to this rule.

    I expected—no, demanded—a fast and efficient recovery. What I got was a slow and sometimes discouraging process that allowed me to develop a better appreciation for good health and good friends. The legendary reporter John Chancellor once observed, *"If you really want to make God laugh, tell him your plans."* I am certain I gave God some good laughs throughout my recovery.

    **What's the big idea?**

    I created a "mantra" that helped me manage my depression: *"I choose to embrace the life I've been given, rather than mourn the life I've lost."* During the really tough times, I probably said this to myself a hundred times each day!

## Five things no man will tell you about prostate cancer:

1. He's scared.
2. He's scared you'll reject him because he's (pick one) incontinent and/ or impotent.
3. He's scared he'll never be able to make love to you again.
4. He's scared the cancer will come back and kill him.
5. He's scared you'll find out he's scared.

# *Day 104*

A celebration.

It is dawning on me that every day is worth celebrating, not just the big days. You can always find a reason to rejoice at Christmas, weddings, anniversaries, graduations, and the like. But, there are a lot of "ordinary" days worth enjoying.

Take today for instance.

Today is Charlotte's birthday—a day she'd probably just as soon forget. That's the way women are with birthdays. It seems that once they achieve adulthood, they'd just as soon not remember them. It's all this "age" thing. I think they worry too much about it.

If you're a PCa survivor and are winding your way through this hellish maze of recovery, each day you're not in chemo is a very good day—a day worth celebrating.

I know I have sounded pessimistic during this recovery. There are days where I can't seem to emerge from the black hole. Days when the continence isn't there and I struggle with my lack of desire for work. And don't get me started about ED. There's a part of my life I may NEVER see again.

What can I do about it?

I am starting to believe that I had better learn to embrace the life I have, rather than mourn the life I've lost. It's better at least to have *half* of something than *all* of nothing. It's a lesson I'm trying to learn—kind of like learning to snow ski. I'm not good at this yet because it is indeed a slippery slope. But, maybe with practice and (wait for it) patience, I'll get better.

Who knows? Perhaps one day I'll be an optimist instead of the cynical pessimist. I'll be a glass-is-half-full guy instead of a glass-is-half-empty guy. It could happen. It could be the mysterious "lesson" that I am supposed to get out of this. Maybe it's a bonus: *I learn to be patient AND optimistic.* It could be kind of a "buy one, get one" deal.

Until I have this revelation—this Aldersgate-type experience[1]—I'll keep applauding birthdays and the life I've been given. I've about decided that life is a lot like birthdays. As long as you have breath to blow out the candles, it's a day worth celebrating.

———

## What you should remember at this point:

1. Your man will go through every stage of grief in no particular order.
2. It's you and him against the disease.
3. Lead, don't push.
4. Depression is normal; deep depression isn't.
5. He's an iceberg—you know only about 10 percent of what he's feeling.
6. Accept him for what he is now—not for what he was or will be.

———

[1] *24th May, 1738*

*At a society near Aldersgate Street, John Wesley experienced his conversion, which he described in his Journal: "In the evening I went very unwillingly to a society in Aldersgate Street, where one was reading Luther's Preface to the Epistle to the Romans. About a quarter before nine, while he was describing the change which God works in the heart through faith in Christ, I felt my heart strangely warmed. I felt I did trust in Christ, Christ alone for salvation; and an assurance was given me that He had taken away my sins, even mine, and saved me from the law of sin and death."*

# Day 104, *continued*

How do you show the woman you love how much you appreciate her support during the worst time of your life? Words aren't enough. I've been blessed. She's met every challenge with equal parts grace and good humor, so this gift had to be special.

This very special gift had a very simple card:

*"I had to get these for you. They reminded me of your eyes when I saw you after surgery."*

Inside the small, red box were two diamond earrings.

They did look like her eyes—sparkling, luminous—eyes that communicated just what the surgeon told her: *"We got it!"*

———

# LIVING LEVITRA LOCA

# CHAPTER 9

# Turn out the lights, the party's *not* over!

## *Day 125*

Charlotte and I continued our recovery world tour this afternoon by going to a movie. We saw *Along Came Polly*. It was a silly romantic comedy that didn't require much thought—kind of like a "summer" movie in the winter. We enjoyed it, but what we enjoyed even more was still more progress in a return to normalcy. Getting out, going places, and doing the things "normal" people do is very important right now. We feel as if we make progress with each step.

Charlotte has wanted "normal" all along.

We both know we lost "normal" the day I was diagnosed, and we've been struggling ever since to get it back. "Normal" to us isn't an exotic ideal, it's just a return to the precancer days when we did things and just lived our lives. Each time we go to the grocery store, office, or dry cleaners, we put "normal" more within our reach. It's still early in the recovery, but I think I see normal off in the distance. I've got to tell you he looks damn good.

———

I have a confession. The *second* thought I had after hearing my diagnosis was that my sex life was going to die (my first thought was that *I* was going to die!). I am pleased to report I was wrong on both counts.

Here's the good news: After you have prostate surgery, the party's not over; but it *is* different. For some guys, prostate surgery is just a blip on the radar. They're back in the saddle in a handful of months. For other guys, recovery of their sexual selves is a much longer process. The reason for all of this is that the nerves controlling erection are located on both sides of the prostate. If the cancer has advanced into these nerves, they will be removed during surgery. If cancer hasn't progressed this far, there's still a chance they may be damaged during the operation. In every case, whether the cancer has spread or not, the nerves will be disturbed. It can take months, even years, to heal adequately. The result can mean anything from short-term erectile dysfunction to long-term impotence.

How you deal with this part of your recovery has a lot to do with the relationship you enjoyed prior to surgery. If you're in a loving, supportive relationship, you have an edge over the other guys. It's important to have a partner who understands both the disease and the impact it can have on a man. It's even more important for you to understand the impact it can have on *you*.

## Developing a Viagrattitude

Immediately following your operation, you will be unable to have an erection. It doesn't mean you won't have feelings or the urge to have one, but you will not be able to achieve an erection suitable for intercourse. Some urologists prescribe an erectile dysfunction (ED) medication for their patients almost immediately after surgery to stimulate blood flow back into the penis. What medicines? You've seen the TV commercials and read the magazine ads—Viagra®, Levitra®, and Cialis® are the three big ED medications. Some work better than others and every man responds differently to different drugs.

Dr. Lee, my Urology Associates of North Texas urologist, took the "cafeteria" approach to ED meds. I was given samples of the three most widely prescribed impotence drugs and encouraged to take them all for a spin. I found that Viagra—at least in my experience—worked best, so my doctor prescribed one 50-mg tablet daily at bedtime.

At first, I was confused by the instructions. I thought Viagra worked only when accompanied by some form of stimulation, and that it should be taken solely as a prelude to intercourse. I was wrong. My doctor ordered the medication for its rehabilitative effect. A recent study backs him up.

Research conducted by Dr. Frank Sommer at the University of Cologne in Cologne, Germany, suggests that nightly treatment may help promote erectile function. His study followed seventy-six men who had erectile dysfunction for at least six months. The first group took 50 mg of Viagra at bedtime each night. The second group took 50–100 mg of Viagra when initiating intercourse. A third group of men with erectile dysfunction received no treatment. All of the men were approximately forty-seven years old.

After one year of nightly Viagra followed by one month of no ED treatment, nearly 60 percent of the men in the first group had normal erections. Only 10 percent of men who took Viagra as needed had a similar return of normal erections. This wasn't a huge study by any definition and it's safe to say the medical community is still debating the effectiveness of this therapy. Your doctor may or may not prescribe post-op ED medication for you, but it wouldn't hurt to ask.

## Day 127–130

Throughout this ordeal that is cancer recovery, I have been wrestling with several conditions. Two of the biggest hurdles have been incontinence and impotence. The two "Is" of prostate cancer surgery are a real bastard. When you throw in the overwhelming depression that accompanies them for good measure, it's a potentially lethal combination of emotions and discomfort all rolled into one nice neat package. Convenient as it sounds, it's a real bitch to deal with.

**What's the big idea?**

If your doctor hasn't prescribed an ED medication (the big three include Viagra, Cialis, and Levitra), ask! Some doctors believe a nightly dose of 50 mg of Viagra, for example, can help restore sexual potency following prostate surgery.

I have been a not-so-patient patient. This stuff would try the patience of Job and, as those of you with any biblical background will remember, Job wasn't really patient. Job and I row the same boat—biblically speaking.

Do I pray?

Sure.

Do I believe prayer is answered?

Er, yeah…but it's never on your time schedule (see Job reference above).

Take impotence as an example.

Dr. Lee put me on 50 mg of Viagra daily to "stimulate the blood flow." I take it at night as directed to try to generate a nighttime erection. It's something all "normal" guys have—just not guys who've recently had their prostate removed.

Like any good patient, I have been patient, routinely taking my medicine each and every night. I see nothing. I experience nothing. I feel nothing. I am convinced that Karl is exacting his perverse revenge on me for throwing him out with the other medical waste the afternoon of December 8. He didn't go gently into that good night and he wants to make sure that I don't forget him. Impotence is his way of telling me that I will forever carry a reminder of him passing through my life.

So what do I do? I take my 50 mg of Viagra each night and I pray.

I don't ask God for an immediate recovery or any special dispensation. I have been asking for the simplest of things: a sign. No burning bush, no angels in the mist telling me not to be afraid…just a sign. Anything to give at least a ray of hope that maybe someday I MIGHT, just might, be able to get this part of my life back. Hey, after all I've been through, I don't think it's asking for much.

This has been my routine since February—each night the same prayer and each night the same answer: nothing.

That is until two nights ago.

I was awakened by the strangest sensation. A feeling I hadn't experienced since before my surgery. It was enough to wake me up: a (very mild) erection.

I was so surprised by this turn of events that I sat up in bed. No, it wasn't a dream.

It was real.

Now, it wasn't "ready for prime time." It would not allow me to have intercourse but it was an actual erection. It'd been so long since I had one that I didn't know what to think. Hell, I didn't even know what to *feel*. After all of this time of taking the drugs and working out with my vacuum erection device I was finally seeing a result.

It wasn't a burning bush. Angels didn't sing.

Nobody handed me any tablets. But for this sit-in-the-back-pew Protestant, it was truly an answered prayer. At least, that's how I interpreted it.

After a couple of minutes of introspection and examination, I thanked God for this feeling that had made my heart race and lifted more than my spirits.

Sign or not, I was grateful. As I rolled over on my right side to drift back to sleep and dream of the promise of a full recovery someday, my "rational" self kicked in.

God couldn't be speaking to me. Could he?

This wasn't him answering my prayer. Was it?

As I was sorting all of this out, I decided to thank God for this amazing feeling.

"*God,*" I said in my half-asleep, half-awake prayer, "*thank you for this amazing feeling and gift of hope. I don't know if you're trying to tell me something,*" I continued, "*but if you are, I want you to know that I appreciate you listening to me for all of these months.*"

As I finished my prayer, I didn't get an answer. In spite of my recent experience, I didn't really expect one. The backsliding Methodist was once again in charge of my groggy brain.

"*One more thing,*" I said as kind of a P.S. to my Creator, "*if this was a sign, it was a really good one.*"

With the thought of a heavenly sign still playing in my head, I opened my eyes one last time and glanced at the clock on the nightstand—12:25 it glowed.

"*Merry Christmas,*" I thought as I drifted back to sleep.

And to all a good night.

---

## The male myth

Some guys think sexual satisfaction is impossible without an erection. That's wrong. An erection *is,* of course, the only way to achieve penetration for intercourse, but it's not the only way to have an orgasm. And neither you nor your partner must have intercourse to be sexually satisfied.

This is a big disconnect for a lot of guys. For some of us, loss of the ability to achieve an erection somehow makes us feel "less" than a man. Don't allow yourself to fall into that trap! Remember chapter 2? *You didn't cause your cancer, so you don't have to feel guilty.*

Think of this as an opportunity to discover a new level of intimacy with your partner. Be creative. Use oral or manual stimulation to bring each other to orgasm. Take the emphasis off erections and penetration and explore each other's wants and needs. Don't overlook the possibility that your partner may actually enjoy (some women actually prefer) intimacy without intercourse. It's another male myth that women must have intercourse to be satisfied. This just isn't true.

If you find yourself at a loss for creative ways to explore this new intimacy, there are plenty of great self-help books available online to avoid embarrassment. The most important lesson to remember is to be supportive. Be sensitive to each other's likes and dislikes, wants and needs. I know you may have a hard time believing this now, but this has the opportunity to take your relationship to an entirely new level. Your sex life might not be like it was in your BC days. It might be *better.*

## Dry orgasm

So, what's it like, this new "intimacy"? Well, as I said, it is *different.*

Regardless of your ability to achieve an erection,

### What's the big idea?

Many insurance plans will pay for only five Viagra tablets each month. You can double the amount they'll pay for by asking your urologist to prescribe 100 mg instead of the typical 50 mg dose. Simply fill your prescription and then cut the 100 mg tablets in half with a pill cutter (cost is less than $5). You'll have ten, 50 mg Viagra tablets for the same price as five.

after prostate surgery you will no longer ejaculate when you orgasm. That walnut-sized prostate gland you once had was the depository for the fluid that carried semen. Now that it's gone, there's no fluid. No fluid...no ejaculation; it's as simple as that.

Will you still have an orgasm? Wow! Yes! You will have a "dry" orgasm. Many prostate cancer survivors will tell you that post-operative orgasms are even more intense than before. It's a little unnerving at first, but you'll get used to it. Your partner may need some education on this point. Since you no longer ejaculate, she may not think you're satisfied. Of course, you'll know you are, but she could probably use some reassurance.

What if you're able to orgasm and be intimate, but you haven't recovered the ability to achieve an erection? In many men, erections will return in time with treatment. Some men never regain potency. Give yourself plenty of time. Think months, not weeks, and you may be surprised at the outcome. If your body's not responding to medication or rehabilitation, it doesn't mean you'll never have another erection. It just means you'll have to explore other options. Here are a couple I've tried.

# Day 132

You're up. You're down.

I know the progress reports that I write sometimes sound alternatively dark and bright. I need to clear up the confusion. It has less to do with common mood swings as it does with the real reason: this is an UP and DOWN disease. I'll explain.

Just when you think you've got it handled, that you're heading the right direction, you get your ass kicked by something you didn't even see coming. Cancer is like that, or so I'm learning. The insidious bastard just lies around and waits for you to feel good, then kicks you in the balls. Karl must be stopped.

I worked at an event yesterday afternoon and early evening for a client (OK, not just any client, but a high-maintenance client). There was a lot of hauling in of materials and rushing around—the usual pre-event stuff. No big deal...no big deal for anyone except me.

I picked up boxes and felt the muscles tighten for the first time in a long time. It didn't really hurt too much. I bent over to pick them up and "Squirt!" It happened each time. As disgusting and humiliating as this was, it's not the really good part.

The meeting began without a hitch. Smooth sailing. I sat there relaxing while the presentation was going on, drinking a glass of iced tea. The presentation ended and I went to the restroom. Careful to go to bathroom stall (urinals weren't designed for prostate cancer guys still wearing pads), I unzipped and began to urinate.

"Bloooop!" was the sound it made when it shot out of my penis. It didn't hurt that much but was unsettling, because there in the water below me was what might best be described as a wad of phlegm. It was white and stringy with a dark "spot" located near the center. It looked like the "white stuff" was wrapping the dark stuff. *"God only knows what that is,"* I thought.

I had a brief thought of trying to retrieve it to see if I could identify it enough to tell Dr. Lee, but it disappeared when someone flushed a urinal. Gone, never to be seen again.

I didn't have any trouble peeing after it was gone. I didn't have any trouble passing it, so I did what any cancer survivor would try to do—put it out of my mind. It's tough to do, but I'm getting better at it.

Someone might ask, *"Why didn't you tell someone? How about your wife?"* To that I would reply, *"Don't you think she's tired of hearing about this?"*

Hey, you're up; you're down.

A former client of mine used to have a saying. The guy manufactured ultralight airplanes—kind of lawn chairs with wings. He was certifiable. I flew with him one time and I still have nightmares.

Before we took off, I asked him what it was like. His reply, *"You never want to fly any higher than you'd like to fall,"* he said.

I am learning that it's the same with cancer.

One day you're flying high. The next day your ass is swinging from a power line.

What a ride!

———

## We're here to pump you up!

I had never heard of a vacuum erection device (VED) before I was diagnosed. Chances are you've never heard of one either. I'll explain.

A VED is a medical device *(most insurance plans will cover at least part of the cost)* that creates a vacuum around the penis and draws blood into the blood vessels so an erection can be achieved. Does it work? Yes, but it takes practice and patience. With proper use, you should be able to produce an erection suitable for intercourse.

The VED is really a simple piece of equipment comprised of three parts: a hollow plastic cylinder, a pump, and a rubber constriction band. The constriction band is placed around the end of the plastic cylinder closest to your body. When the cylinder is placed over the penis, the user simply "pumps" the handle to create a vacuum. The vacuum creates a suction that pulls blood into the blood vessels in the penis. When an erection is achieved, you simply slide the rubber constriction band off the cylinder and on to the erect penis. You're now ready for "normal" intercourse.

A VED erection will be maintained even through orgasm. When you are through having sex, you simply remove the constriction band and the penis returns to its normal state. It's simple.

I strongly urge you to read the instructions carefully (some even come with a video). Most will stress that erections lasting longer than thirty minutes can be harmful. If you decide to take this route, don't go crazy. A VED is a very good solution to erectile dysfunction, but don't overdo it.

This is a low-tech way to get back in the game. Sure, it's a little more complicated than taking a pill but it does have advantages. The VED allows you to be "master of your domain" once more. And the ability to achieve an erection anytime you want—for as long as you want (again, follow label directions)—is exciting.

# Day 137

It *really* sucks.

Yes, the vacuum erection device (VED) really *does* suck. That's what it's supposed to do. Today I found out...well, sort of. At least, I had an appointment with the "physical therapist/salesman" that reps these devices. We met at Dr. Lee's office. It all had a "clinical" feel to it—kind of hard (well, not really) to get hard in that kind of environment.

I met Raymond *("Call me Ray")*, the "therapist," in an exam room and he walked me through the intricacies of the device in about fifteen minutes. He showed me how the VED worked and demonstrated it using the palm of his hand (it left a good hickey). I couldn't help but think as he went through his demo what his day must be like. His entire vocation is dedicated to helping guys get erections.

When he isn't talking about penises, he's working with them. What kind of ad did he answer to get this job? "DOES YOUR JOB SUCK? THIS ONE DOES! Professional wanted to train men in the use of vacuum erection devices. Must be able to use the words 'penis,' 'pubic hair,' 'testes,' and 'lubricant' without busting a gut laughing. Experience helpful, but not required. Call 1-800-BIG-DICK for more information."

Something tells me the *Dallas Morning News* would never run that ad.

I'll say this for him; the guy's a pro. He had me signed up by the end of the session. Soon, I'll be getting a (plain brown?) package from UPS. It'll contain my VED, tension rings, a video, and maybe even some complimentary lube. I can't wait to try it out. If it works, I may not applaud. But I will give a standing ovation.

---

## Take your best shot!

Another solution to erectile dysfunction is penile injection.

I know what you're thinking: *"I could NEVER give myself a shot there!"* Many men feel that way. I've seen guys as tough as a Texas boot shudder at the mention of this option. But, like a lot of things associated with this disease, it's not as bad as you might think.

Penile injection medication comes in several different forms, but the two most popular are Caverject and Tri-Mix. Typically, your urologist will discuss this option with you and arrange an appointment for an in-office injection. Your doctor will give you the first shot so he can monitor the dose and the duration of your erection. If everything works to his and your satisfaction, you'll be given a prescription and instructed on how to inject yourself.

It sounds a lot more complicated than it really is. The tricky part of penile injections is getting the dosage right. It can take a surprisingly small amount of medicine to achieve an erection that will last for hours (*this isn't a typo—I said, hours!*). Getting the correct dose takes some practice, but the results are worth it.

In addition to getting the dosage right, there's another trick to penile injections: the actual injection itself. First of all, don't let the needle throw you. You'll use a diabetic syringe so the needle is incredibly thin, sharp, and short (about a one-half inch). After the initial shock of learning how to inject yourself, you'll find that it's just about pain free.

The inside trick to penile injections is using an auto injector so you don't actually have to "stick" yourself with a needle.

What's an "auto injector"?

It's a small, spring-loaded plastic device that looks like a hollowed-out, plastic ballpoint pen. It holds a fully loaded syringe but the needle is completely covered, so you never see it.

After placing the syringe into the auto injector, you simply put it on the shaft of your penis and push the button. The spring-loaded injector "injects" the medication quickly, easily, and painlessly. All you have to do is push the plunger on the syringe and remove it when you're through.

There are several automatic injectors on the market. The B-D Inject-Ease Automatic Injector (about $25) works great and there are others that will also do the job. If you're the least bit squeamish about injecting yourself, I strongly recommend this device.

## What's the big idea?

If you take the injection route, be sure to have some Sudafed—the version that contains the medicine ephedrine—on hand. If you experience a prolonged erection, a dose of Sudafed may stop it and save you a trip to the emergency room.

Injections aren't for everyone. However, if you're not satisfied with the results you get from pills and pumps, you should discuss this alternative with your physician. Don't let the fear of injecting yourself keep you from exploring this option. Anyone can do it with an automatic injector.

## What you should remember at this point:

1. You don't need an erection to be sexually satisfied.
2. You'll still have orgasms and they'll be more intense.
3. If your doctor hasn't prescribed an ED medication, ask!
4. Discuss the vacuum erection device (VED) with your physician.
5. Penile injections are easier than you think and auto injectors make them virtually pain free.

# Day 150

Practice makes erections?

Well, that's what the manual says at least.

I have gotten better at this pumping thing, but I'm still a long way from lift off. Yeah, it does increase (dramatically) the blood flow to the penis. Yes, it does make it semierect. Yes, I think (with time) it will allow me to have an erection. Who knows? With enough practice and (wait for it) TIME and PATIENCE, I may be able to have an erection without it someday.

When will that day come?

Perhaps it's better to say, *"If that day comes..."* Do I sound a little dejected? Hell yeah! But then, let me ask you, would YOU be dejected if YOU were dealing with incontinence and impotence at the EXACT SAME TIME? ONE of these is enough to make most men so depressed they consider running off to Alaska. I'm with TWO. For those of you scoring at home, this is difficult—kind of like executing a double backflip while wearing a space suit.

This "practice" has now become part of my daily routine. I run in the mornings and before I shower, I "pump it up." It's not terribly unpleasant but it does take some getting used to. I may never get used to it, but I'll do it until I have an erection or die trying. Wouldn't that make an interesting conversation?

*"How did your first husband die, Mrs. Hill?"* they'd ask.

*"Well he was using his vacuum erection device and blew the head right off his penis. Stupid bastard bled to death before we could get him to the hospital."*

They'd nod sympathetically and then ask her out. Me? I'd be forever known as the guy who blew his dick off.

You have to admit, it would make for one funny obituary.

———

.

# CHAPTER 10

# Embracing the new "normal"

## Day 156

Back to normal?

We planted flowers today. Charlotte and I went to the nursery and bought about 280 pansies (oddly enough, a lot less than we've done in years past). We worked outside most of the day, because it was sunny and the upper seventies. A little windy, but pretty weather for planting.

At the end of the day, we were a little tired and a little sore. We were happy with the job we'd done.

*"I'm sorry for making you do all of this,"* Charlotte said as we got into bed.

*"You didn't make me do anything I didn't want to do. I'm glad we planted everything. It looks nice,"* I offered.

*"I just wanted to make things normal. To do the things we'd ordinarily do at this time of year. It felt good to be outside. It felt good to forget for a little while,"* she added.

*"Yeah,"* I said, *"it felt good."*

Normal? Back to normal? When will that come? I think we'll never see normal again. Normal is a memory and it's fading fast.

There'll be a new "normal" and I can't begin to describe what that will be like. All I know is that it will be different. Charlotte tells me that "different" doesn't always mean "bad." I hope she's right.

———

Almost from the very first day of my diagnosis, my wife has said the same thing: *"Just because it's different doesn't mean it's bad."* She's said it so often it's almost become a catchphrase. The truth is she's right.

It's a powerful statement. Right now, they are just words on a page to you. The day you can fully accept this idea, you will truly be on your way to recovery.

Most guys don't handle change very well. I know I don't. I think a big part of my problem with prostate cancer was that I really don't like change at all. I don't enjoy having to get used to different things. Prostate cancer, however, doesn't give you a choice. It's a lesson I learned the hard way. In fact, I had such a hard time with it that I really couldn't even say "different," so I came up with my own term for it. *Different* is what I ultimately named the *"new normal."*

For prostate cancer survivors, the "new normal" is a very long way from the old normal. How is it different? As you've read, you'll go through different stages in your recovery. At each step, you'll learn something new. You'll pass through some stages quickly (catheter), but others may take a little longer (incontinence), and some may last for a very long time (impotence). At each of these points, you'll learn how to deal with your body, your emotions, and your outlook on life. You'll be surprised how quickly you become accustomed to things you never thought you would, or could, do. Human beings are adaptable creatures. It's a part of our survival instinct. You'll be amazed at what you can learn to do and ultimately accept as normal.

# Day 167

The trouble with normal…as I see it, there are several problems with this disease. Here are three:

1. You don't know how long the recovery will take—there's no way of knowing when you'll get back to "normal."
2. There's no way of knowing IF you'll ever get back to "normal."
3. If you make your way back to "normal," you never know how long it may last.

You see, when you break your leg or have some stitches, the doctor can give you the usual four- to six-week timeframe. Each day, you see progress and, lo and behold, in that time frame, you're actually healed.

It doesn't work that way with prostate cancer. You just never know if that day will come. It's like waiting for Christmas to arrive, except you're unsure if Christmas will actually come this year. It's frustrating and often depressing. Just when you think Christmas is here, you discover someone moved the date. For some guys, prostate cancer means Christmas never comes.

Some survivors wonder (myself included) if they will ever get back to normal. What you find out—understanding, of course, that surgery had a positive outcome—is that "normal" is different, vastly different, from what you've ever experienced. In other words, it's not the "normal" you expect, it's the "normal" you get. I guess you get used to it so the "new normal" becomes "normal." In any case, it's what you get, so it really doesn't matter.

Then there's the not knowing how long normal will last. No one ever really says they're "cured" from cancer. Doctors won't ever tell you you're cured. They'll talk in terms of five-year, ten-year, and fifteen-year "survival rates." From what I can tell, the odds are about 50/50 that Karl will pay a return visit and kick my ass.

———

The important thing to remember about the new normal is that you have to accept it for what it is and get on with your life. I'm not suggesting you give up...absolutely not! But, I am saying you should approach each stage with the attitude of trying to learn something from it. Incontinence taught me control. Impotence

## What's the big idea?

I've always heard that successful athletes have the ability to "visualize" sinking the putt or hitting the winning home run. You can do that too. At each stage of your recuperation, try imagining yourself at the next point. You'll be surprised at the change it will make in your attitude and how it will help your recovery progress.

taught me patience. Each stage was a lesson in appreciation for things I once took for granted. What was formerly automatic suddenly became manual. I had to work at everything and I celebrated whatever success I accomplished.

I ultimately embraced the new normal and tried to learn every lesson so I could use it further down the line.

## Getting from never to forever

So, how do you embrace the new normal? Well, it's a five-step process and the first trick is getting to "someday." I'll explain.

The first and least hopeful of these stages is "never." That's where we all begin. When you were first diagnosed, you were really depressed and you probably said something like: *"I'll never have a normal sex life."* As you continued your recovery and your body began to heal, it's likely you became more optimistic. At that point, you began to see a glimmer of hope. You went from saying, *"I'll never have a normal sex life again"* to *"Someday I'll have a normal sex life."*

Do you see the difference? Getting from "never" to "someday" is a HUGE step. To reach this point, you have to be able to see yourself achieving that goal. I know it sounds trite, but if you believe in "someday," you'll be surprised at how much more hopeful your life will become.

Getting to step three is an exercise in even more confidence.

Step three is "soon." This requires a little optimism and a lot more faith. Soon means change is just around the bend. Most guys can see "soon" when their recovery has passed some imaginary milestone. My "soon" came when I was waging my battle with incontinence. I thought I would "never" become continent again. Slowly—sometimes, it was like watching a glacier move—I walked toward regaining my continence. It was easier to chart progress here because I measured it in the number of incontinence pads I used each day. It began with four to five daily and slowly worked its way to three to four. When I rounded the corner to two, I began thinking "soon." Soon, for me at least, was another two months. But it was this belief in "soon" that helped me find the next step.

"Now" is the next-to-last step in embracing change. It's probably the trickiest stop on this tour. Why? Because it's so difficult to predict just when "now" is going to happen. The lesson here is that "now" is really just a leap of faith.

I'll give you an example.

I was probably fully continent a good two to three weeks earlier than when I believed it because I was afraid of going "pad free." I was scared that I would have an "accident" and embarrass myself. I was afraid to attempt it so I just didn't try. There was no single moment that caused me to ditch pads entirely and give it shot. I just screwed up my courage one day and said to hell with it. I decided that "now" was the time and I went for it.

I ditched the pads when I got home after work. I went for a couple of hours without them the first day. On the second day, I took it to about four hours. Then I went all night without a pad. My never-someday-soon had finally become NOW. It was an amazing feeling, but it wasn't achieved without screwing up my courage and taking a chance. This risk led me to the final stop in accepting change: forever.

"Forever," is the ultimate destination. It's from this mountaintop that you can finally see just how far you've traveled. What you need to know about "forever" is that it isn't really a destination at all.

It's an attitude.

At this stage in your journey, are you cancer free? If so, do you think you'll be cancer free…forever? The honest answer is "who knows?" But you do have a choice. You can either believe that you'll remain free of the disease, or you can look over your shoulder for the rest of your life, always imagining what it would be like to start over, to go back to "never."

What's it going to be for you: never or forever?

Embrace change at each step and use the experiences to bridge you from one point to the next. Then whatever you do, don't look back.

# Day 181 to 182

Another anniversary.

I've reached the five-month milestone. It is getting harder and harder for me to believe that I had surgery five months ago. In some ways, it seems like only yesterday. In other ways, it seems as if it was years ago. My body knows differently and it finds subtle and not-so-subtle ways of reminding me.

So, where am I now that I've hit the five-month mile marker? Roll call, if you please:

- Incontinence. A huge leap forward has occurred just in the past week. Just when I thought I might never be able to escape pads and liners, I suddenly have hope that someday (?) it might just be a bad memory. For the time being, I'm keeping my fingers (and legs!) crossed.
- ED. It's like the reverse of the old adage, "the mind is willing, but the body is weak." I have zero activity in this area without the use of my VED. If this thing ever breaks down on me, I'm out of business. Charlotte is helpful and encouraging, and she tells me constantly not to be frustrated. My plan right now is to make it to 100 percent continence and then attack the third horseman of the prostate cancer apocalypse head on. I have ED in my sights and I'll come after him next with everything I have.
- Energy. No problems here. I am back to running eight miles a week. I think it has helped me regain my continence and I know it's boosted my energy. Next step: running to the office like I used to. I'll do it soon.
- Attitude. I have good days and bad days. Thanks to my increasing continence, there are more good days than bad. I still get depressed (especially around PSA test time), but most days I try not to think about it. It's not that I am putting it out of my mind; it's that I am trying to stay focused and positive about my future. I figure that if I can envision a future without prostate cancer, I might just be able to have one.
- Pain. Gone. Zip. Zero. Nada. The only real pain I feel is when I push myself too hard exercising. Other than that, most of the scars are beginning to disappear (all expect my two largest ones). Inside, I guess I'm

OK; there haven't been any "incidents" for the past two months. I guess I've peed about everything out that I'm going to pee out. You might say I've "passed" that test!

I've created a daily mantra for myself that seems to help, both spiritually and physically: *"I choose to embrace the life I've been given, rather than mourn the life I've lost."* I repeat it to myself each day and whenever I see Karl staring at me in my rearview mirror. Life is good. You just have to remind yourself from time to time.

I have resolved to keep positive (OK, I let myself get down occasionally, but not like before) and to keep focused on the good things. As Dr. Lee said to me at my first checkup, *"Don't worry, Mr. Hill, I'll have you as a neighbor for many, many years."*

You know what?

I'm beginning to think he may be right. We both have a lot of anniversaries in our futures.

———

## What you should remember at this point:
1. Just because it's different doesn't mean it's bad.
2. Embrace change.
3. Learn a little more each day.
4. Have the courage to fail.
5. Don't look back.

# Day 275

Charlotte and I were making our first cross-country road trip after surgery and we talked about my recovery and how we were handling it.

*"Do you ever have a day when you don't think about this?"* she asked.

*"I like to focus on the future,"* I said. *"The other stuff depresses me."*

*"Like what?"* she asked.

*"Impotence. It makes me so frustrated..."* I said, my voice drifting off until it was completely covered by the whine of the tires on the dry pavement.

*"What does Dr. Lee say?"* she continued, trying not to sound too concerned.

*"He says it could take up to thirty-six months. After that it's anyone's guess,"* I said.

*"It's early then,"* she said. *"Give it time."*

*"But, if you really push him he'll say, 'Mr. Hill, I am sorry. We had to take one-half of your nerves in the surgery. We did our best."*

*"So, what does that mean?"* she asked.

*"It means we'll have to wait and see,"* I added.

*"Is 'wait and see' OK, with you?"* she said.

*"It'll have to be,"* I said. *"I'm fairly happy with my progress, but unfortunately the surgery wasn't complete."*

*"Wasn't complete?"* she said. *"What didn't they get?"*

*"My memories,"* I answered. *"I remember what it was like in BC—Before Cancer. I want things back the way they were, at least the way they were without cancer."*

*"Those were good times,"* she said. *"We'll have plenty more. Wait and see."*

With those words, she confirmed what I suspected for some time. Charlotte had fully embraced the "new normal" of life after prostate cancer. She hadn't just accepted it; she had wrapped her arms around it and had it in a big bear hug. I knew that soon there wouldn't be a "new normal," there would be only the "normal" that we had built for ourselves, like settlers in the New World.

We continued our drive that afternoon. As we sped past the fields and farmhouses of Mississippi, I thought that Charlotte was probably right. It was time to embrace the "new normal" and disconnect from the "old." It wasn't coming back anyway. The future lay ahead of us like the slender ribbon of road that would carry us home. The old BC days grew dim in the rearview mirror. Soon, very soon, we wouldn't see them at all.

———

# CHAPTER 11

# The price *isn't* right

## Day 280

The price you pay.

When I first learned that Karl was paying me a visit, I drew some comfort in the fact that I had good insurance. Best of all, I thought to myself, I even have supplemental cancer insurance. We bought it years ago. And when I learned about my unfortunate circumstance, I felt good knowing I'd at least hedged my bet.

It turned out to more of a shrub than a hedge.

I received a whopping $2,360. Not an insignificant windfall, but just barely enough to cover my out-of-pocket deductible. In short, my "supplement" when all the bills are paid will pretty much bring me back to even.

So much for pain and suffering!

Of course, you have to ask yourself if you can really put a price on something like this. I rationalize the fact that you can't.

Cancer really does get its pound of flesh from you. It exacts a toll. Me? All I have to put up with is incontinence and the loss of spontaneous intimacy.

I shouldn't complain, should I?

It all comes down to value and values. I guess if you value your life, there's no cost too great, no price too steep. If you don't have to go through chemotherapy, there's no amount of money that you'd accept to go through it.

Yeah, cancer is expensive.

The lucky ones are the guys who are still around to pay the price.

———

You've known from the very beginning that cancer would exact a price on you. About the only thing in question was just how much you'd pay. Does it really matter? Can you put a price on being cancer free? Don't even try.

There are others, however, who will put a price on your diagnosis, treatment, and recovery. Insurance companies are in the business of calculating the cost of every aspect of this disease. They can tell you to the penny what a radical prostatectomy is worth and what they'll pay. You can only go along for the ride. Right? That's not entirely true.

It's up to you—the informed patient—to look out for yourself and make sure you don't pay more than you owe. If you're not careful, it's entirely possible that you will. Here's how you can avoid that happening.

# Three Tricks for Handling Health Insurance

## Trick #1

### Keep everything and keep it organized

From the moment you leave the hospital, you will be buried in paper. You'll come home with aftercare instructions, phone numbers, and copies of forms you signed. Then the real flood will start. Each day, the letter carrier will bring you another mountain of insurance forms, form letters, and bills from everyone. You've probably already paid your doctor and the hospital, at least in part. But you and your insurance company will still need to settle up with the anesthesiologist, the lab, the assisting surgeon, and others.

Whatever you do, don't throw anything away. File everything. Keeping good records is the first step in ensuring you pay only the bills you're supposed to pay. As you've already discovered, hospitals are big, busy places. It's easy for mistakes to be made. You need a paper trail to protect yourself in the event a mistake is made that could cost you. It's just as important to protect your *fiscal* health as it is to protect your *physical* health.

Keep every copy of every invoice you receive, even if the invoices show you owe nothing. If you have some basic computer skills, create a spreadsheet to keep track of this mountain of paperwork. If you're not computer savvy, invest in a big three-ring binder, a hole punch, and some divider tabs so you can keep everything together. Then, if there's a problem, it'll be easy for you to find the answer you need to help resolve it.

You'll need to keep track of everything for a year or even longer. I received my last invoice thirteen months *after* my surgery. In fact, the invoice was so "old" the insurance company initially refused to pay because it was beyond its time limit. They finally paid the bill—a radiologist invoice for an X-ray—but not without a fight. Hang on to your records for at least two years. You'll be glad you did.

# Trick #2

## You're responsible so behave responsibly

Among the dozens of forms you signed before surgery, one made you the guarantor for the services about to be performed on you. In plain English it means you're financially responsible, even if the insurance company decides not to pay.

Now, I'm not suggesting that insurance companies don't pay—I have plenty of friends in the insurance industry. What I am saying is that big insurance companies didn't get to be big insurance companies without being scrupulous caretakers of the money you've paid in premiums all these years. They're very careful about who gets paid, what gets paid, and when it gets paid. You can get caught in the middle, lodged between an insurance company's accounts payable, and a hospital's accounts receivable. It's not a fun spot.

If you find yourself here, be patient. Be polite. But, most importantly be firm, and don't be quick writing a check. Insurance companies operate on their own timetable and sometimes it can seem sluggish, even to hospitals that are used to slow-paying insurance companies. If you feel threatened or a little overwhelmed by all of this, pick up the phone, call your insurance company's customer service line, and explain the situation. Believe me, they've heard it all before and will probably be able to help you resolve the problem. Even if they're no help, make a note for your records with the date, time, and purpose of your call. Also, record whom you talked with and what you discussed.

Should you feel the need to pay an invoice from one of your caregivers and "settle up later" with the insurance company, beware. If you think it takes a long time for them to pay hospitals and doctors who are contract vendors, just imagine how long it could take you to receive reimbursement. My advice: don't do it.

Above all, keep your cool. Return any phone calls you receive from hospital or physician billing departments. Don't take the attitude that *"the insurance company is handling this, why should I get involved?"* Keep good records of these conversations as well. These important matters could jeopardize your credit if you're not careful.

It's unlikely this will happen, but if you find yourself in the unfortunate position of getting calls from bill collectors regarding invoices, it may be time to pay a visit to the hospital accounting office. Be polite. Explain the facts and bring your records with you. People—even people in the accounts receivable office trying to collect past-due amounts—are still people like you and me. Sit down with them and explain the situation using your records to show the facts. Nobody wants to ruin your credit or go unpaid. You may be surprised at what you're able to work out. It's human nature. Most people are willing to help others when given the opportunity.

# Trick #3

## Be creative

It's likely your doctor will prescribe one of the erectile dysfunction (ED) drugs during your recovery. The idea is for the medicine to stimulate the blood flow back into your penis. It all sounds like good, rational medicine doesn't it? Jump-starting your member seems like a smart idea, but there's one problem. Your well-meaning, premiums-paid-in-full health insurance company doesn't look at it that way. For all they know, you're a practicing porn star (yeah, they'd think differently if they'd examine your records and see your recent bill for prostate surgery, but they won't.)

Your urologist will likely prescribe an every-other-day dose of one of the better-known ED drugs. The only problem with that prescription is that your health insurance probably won't cover it. At best, they'll likely pay for only five pills per month. Any way you do the math, five pills per month won't cover an every-other-day prescription. What do you do?

Be creative.

The funny thing about health insurance companies is that they don't seem to care about the dosage; they only want to limit how many pills you receive.

Make sure your doctor prescribes at least ten pills per month. If your health insurance provider pays for only five Viagra, for example, you may have to pay out-of-pocket for the remaining five in order to get the ten pills you need to make it through the month.

Now, here's the really important part.

Ask your physician to write the prescription dosage for *twice* the amount he wants you to take. For example, if your doctor prescribes one, 25 mg Viagra every other day, ask him to write your prescription for 50 mg Viagra.

When you pick up your prescription, purchase a "pill splitter" (about $5). Then, when you get home with your ten 50 mg Viagra, cut them in half with the pill splitter. You now have the twenty, 25 mg tabs you need for your every-other-day prescription.

Be sure and tell your doctor what you're doing, but it's unlikely he'll care if you split the ED pills in half. The bottom line is that the insurance company pays what they agreed to pay and you get the pills you need for your recovery. It's not pretty, but it is an effective way to get the medicine you need.

## More insurance is better, right?

Are cancer insurance policies worth it? I'll answer this question with a question. Do you have "wheel" insurance for your car?

Why then, is it a good idea to buy your health insurance one piece at a time? The only place a la carte makes sense is in a restaurant. Cancer insurance is the health provider equivalent of "do you want fries with that?" I had a cancer policy from one of the more reputable companies out there and (buyer beware) it was lousy.

My entire procedure—from diagnosis through recovery—cost approximately $40,000. My primary insurance, which had negotiated contracts with the hospitals and doctors, paid about $20,000. My secondary policy (specifically for cancer) paid about 10 percent of that (a little over $2,000). Was it worth it? My annual premium was more than what I was reimbursed for the pleasure of having the number two killer of adult males in this country. No, I don't think I got my money's worth.

It's up to you to make an informed decision—something worth investigating if you have children, because they are two to five times more likely to have cancer since it is in your family. As for me, I'll pass.

# *Day 287*

The longer I survive cancer, the more I am convinced that there is only one secret to this disease. Do you want to know what it is?

It's simple, really. I'm surprised that no one from Johns Hopkins or MD Anderson has figured this out. This may get me a Nobel Prize in medicine, and I'll reveal it here for the very first time.

**The secret to surviving cancer is just to outlive it.**

Sounds simple, right? Well, there are literally millions who have passed on that will tell you it's anything BUT easy. It's damn hard. For some, it's impossible.

I don't think it's in the recovery really. From what I've read, no doctor will ever tell you that you're "cured" of cancer—"survival rates," that's what they call them. You don't ever beat cancer; you fall into one of the survival groups that medical researchers and statisticians love.

Me, I'm trying to make it through the first group. Right now, I'm on the five-year plan. That's me. The doctors and researchers will tell you that for my age and stage of disease, my chance of "surviving" for at least five years is a whopping 97 percent. Whew! Sounds good, right?

Well, it *does* sound good. And it's only the first leg of the marathon that I have to run to actually be a survivor. For those of you keeping score at home, a true cancer survivor is someone who lives long enough for something OTHER than cancer to kill him or her.

That's my goal.

I want to thumb my nose at Karl as they carry me off to my final reward. I want to string enough days together so I can say that he didn't get me.

That's really all I want.

I just want to live my life.

That's what being a "survivor" is about.

———

## What you should remember at this point:
1. Keep all paperwork for two years.
2. It's your party and you're responsible for the check.
3. Be polite. Be firm. But, most of all be patient.
4. Never pay a bill for your insurance company expecting reimbursement later.
5. If health insurance providers were creative, they wouldn't be health insurance providers. It's up to you to figure out how to get the most from the system you've been paying into for all of these years.

## The eight life lessons of prostate cancer

# Day 290
The short drive home…

Yesterday, as I turned into the neighborhood, I looked into my rearview mirror and saw someone I hadn't seen in a while: Dr. Lee. He was on his way home too. Just us two guys heading home to dinner.

I was having pork chops slow-cooked in mushroom soup. I didn't know what Dr. Lee, his wife, and two children were having for supper, but it was probably something good.

Dinner or not, it wasn't very significant. The important thing was the "normalcy" of it all. The "new normal" that I often imagined had suddenly become real and it stared at me in my rearview mirror. Sure, I've been going to work now for some time since my surgery, but it's amazing how easily you slip back into the routine. Today, that routine became SO routine that it sneaked up on me as I turned down my street.

It was an ordinary day, made not so ordinary by the image I saw in my mirror. Here was another father coming home from a long day at the office. The only difference was this dad had spent his day slicing guys open and doing everything possible to kick cancer's ass. I guessed he had probably kicked a lot of cancer-ass since he cut Karl out of me. I could only hope that the other hundred or so guys who had gone to sleep on his watch had awakened to the news that greeted me: *"We got it."* Three magical words that can make you dance even when you can't sit up.

I turned down my street as he turned down his. Ahead of me lay the "new normal" and dinner with my family. I could only guess that Dr. Lee was still enjoying the "normal" of his life. At least up until this point, he hadn't experienced the "new normal" that comes with cancer. My prayer was that he never would. The world needs guys like him that spend their days on the other side of the knife and then go home to carve the pot roast.

As I turned into my driveway, I knew what I'd seen. I'd seen my past. It was there in a white SUV with a hospital parking pass dangling from its rearview mirror. Dr. Lee knew where he was going. He had a pass to take him there. I could only guess where the future would take me. But, I reasoned that as long as I had guys like him watching my back, I could find my way home.

———

1. **Cancer can kill you.**

   I know that's obvious, but what I didn't know when the year began is just how widespread a disease it is. Prostate cancer alone is the number two cancer killer of men behind lung cancer. In the year since I had surgery, some 192,280 men were diagnosed with the disease and about 27,360 of them have stepped on a rainbow (to borrow a line from my favorite country singer, mystery writer, and the man who may be governor of the great state of Texas someday, Kinky "Big Dick" Friedman).

2. **Friends can save you.**

   I don't know how I could have made it without my friends. It would have been nearly impossible for my family to pull through. They were absolute pillars of strength.

3. **Prayer can heal you.**

   I'll be the first to admit that I'm the poster boy for backsliding Methodists, but I have come to believe that prayers are not only answered, they're welcomed by our creator. I secretly think he likes the dialog—kind of like a mother wondering why her son hasn't called in such a long time. I dialed up the deity plenty during the past year and never got voice mail.

4. **Your instinct is still the best guide.**

   Follow your gut. When they remove it, follow your heart. Listen to what the experts say, and if their advice makes sense, don't look back. Remember Lot's wife. She was a pillar of the community, but you wouldn't want to be like her.

5. **Know that you don't know everything, and don't be afraid to admit it.**

   See #4.

6. **Stretch a little each day.**

   The recovery pace can seem almost glacial, but if you put in a marker and look back, you'll be amazed at how far you've come.

7. **Keep your sense of humor.**

   There's something funny in everything if you just look hard enough. Make a game out of finding the funny and you'll be rewarded every time, even if you're the only one laughing.

8. **Never, never, never give up.**

   Cancer survivors have a saying, "Don't give up five minutes before the miracle." They're right.

# *Day 295*

Exam room #4…

I saw Dr. Lee for my checkup. How'd I do?

I'm two for two.

My PSA was <0.1, which, as Dr. Lee so succinctly put it, *"is exactly what we were shooting for."*

Dr. Lee didn't seem to mind that he ended a sentence with a preposition. I didn't mind either. Preposition or not, he was right. It was what I *was* shooting *for*.

There is a curious aspect to this disease.

Let's be clear on something right off the bat. Prostate cancer is *not* a disease at all. It's more like a death sentence with a built-in reprieve. Now that I'm post-op, I go before the judge every ninety days. Some guys (like me so far) beat the rap. Other guys have to serve time in chemo hell. Some guys pass Go and become backup singers for Elvis. It's all in how the cards get cut.

As for me, every ninety days I go down to my friendly neighborhood phlebotomist and they draw enough of my blood to give Dracula a hearty snack. Then they check to see if my PSA is rising (which would mean that Karl has awakened from his nap and is coming back to kick my ass) or, if—as I found out today—Karl is on hiatus. He may be in the Bahamas or Bosnia, but he ain't making time with my corpuscles.

I'll send you a postcard, Karl, you unrighteous bastard.

My visits with Dr. Lee during our every-ninety-day ritual have been routine so far. I come loaded with four or five questions scribbled on a wadded-up yellow Post-It note. Since my body didn't come with an owner's manual, it's the only way I can even attempt to figure out how I'm doing and what may be around the corner.

I usually begin with a status report to Dr. Lee so he can get an idea of what I'm doing and (I hope) tell me if I'm doing something stupid. Here's how our session went.

*"How are you doing?"* Dr. Lee asked as he entered exam room #4 in his starched white doctor's jacket.

*"Good,"* I said, *"pretty good. I'm running eight miles a week."* I wanted to show him that even an old prostate cancer survivor could still pick 'em up and put 'em down. *"I'm even thinking about running a mini marathon—a 5K really—something that would challenge me."*

*"Sounds great,"* he replied, glancing at my patient satisfaction survey that I just filled out in his waiting room. He looked down at me and his demeanor changed when he flipped over to page two.

*"I'd say that for continence I'm about ninety-five percent there,"* I said.

*"As for erections…nothing,"* I continued.

Dr. Lee frowned. He even looked a little sad.

*"Dr. Lee,"* I continued, *"I couldn't get it up if I slammed it in a car door!"* I laughed.

*"Sounds painful,"* he said, *"but, an unforgettable visual."*

*"Don't worry. I won't be doing that anytime soon,"* I said.

We both laughed at my inability to achieve an erection. Ah, impotence humor, you just can't beat it. Well, you *could* but it still wouldn't stand up.

Our conversation then shifted to what I could do to make things better—all really wonderful options:

1. Inject my penis with a chemical solution
2. Insert a tablet into my urethra using a plastic applicator

3. Continue using my VED
4. Wait it out
5. Any combination

After a little debate, I chose option 5. For those of you keeping score at home, this means I'll pretty much keep doing what I've been doing.

*"You know you're really early in the process,"* Dr. Lee said, consoling me.

*"So what am I looking at here?"* I asked.

*"Eighteen to thirty-six months,"* he said. *"Some guys even start experiencing erections beyond that time frame. But basically..."* he trailed off.

*"If it's not up in three years it's not coming up,"* I offered.

*"Right,"* he said.

*"I don't think you'll fall into that category,"* he said, sounding more than a little chipper. We then discussed how the pills had been working—Viagra, Cialis, Levitra. Their names sounded like the chorus in a Greek tragedy.

I left with a handful of pharmaceutical samples. I thanked him as I walked out of exam room #4.

*"Thanks for everything, Dr. Lee,"* I said. *"You're the best."*

*"No, Mr. Hill. No,"* he said shaking his head. He's a modest man and I think probably a little shy.

*"See you in three months?"* I asked.

*"Three months,"* he said.

I walked down the hallway to the front desk. Along the way, I passed men much older than me. Some were walking erect and others trudged down the hall in the stoop-shouldered shuffle I did when I came in with a catheter bag strapped to my leg. I knew what they were going through and winced at the memory.

I filled out my paperwork and spoke to the man behind me. He was one of the younger ones, about fifty-five, maybe a little older.

*"This place is stacked up like DFW Airport,"* I said, making casual conversation. He sat there staring into space. I couldn't tell if he'd just been diagnosed or if something else had happened to him. Whatever it was, it didn't appear to be good news. He wasn't in the mood to pass the time

while the nurse printed out my lab request. The ticket I would need for my next visit to the judge.

*"Yeah, the place is busy…"* he said with a voice that trailed off into the hustle of the hallway, *"real busy."*

I picked up my paperwork and walked through the lobby. Men in their sixties, seventies, and eighties sat there trying to appear interested in old magazines they weren't really reading. Some were with their wives. Some were alone. All had the *look*. Each was waiting his turn.

*"Maybe they'll get exam room #4,"* I thought as I walked out the door. *"It's been good to me."*

———

# Frequently asked questions

1. **How much time do I have before I have to make a decision?**

   It depends on the stage you are diagnosed. Prostate cancer is typically very slow growing, so your doctor will usually counsel you to take some time and make the decision that's best for you. We're talking weeks—and in some cases even months—before you have to do anything. There's even a "watchful waiting" option, where men will wait *years* before taking action. There's normally no need to rush into anything.

2. **Is the surgery painful?**

   Not really. On a scale of one to ten, with ten being excruciating, I'd peg it at a six immediately following surgery. It then decreases rapidly (within an hour or so after coming out from the anesthesia) down to a four or three. By the time you're released from the hospital, it will be in the two to three range. The prescribed pain medication makes the most difficult period manageable. Then, usually within a few days, you'll be back on over-the-counter medicines like Tylenol or Advil.

3. **What DON'T the doctors tell you about this surgery?**

   It's not that they *don't* tell you...it's really more a matter of your know-ing enough to ask more in-depth questions. They'll treat you as if you're on a "need-to-know" basis. If you ask, you need to know, and they'll tell you. They won't volunteer much more than the basics.

4. **Can I expect any post-surgical problems?**

   It's possible, but it doesn't happen often. You'll undergo a complete work-up prior to surgery to ensure you're fit for the operation. Of course, infection is always a risk, and you might develop a low-grade fever for a few days. If you're worried about something in particular, it's important to discuss your concerns with your physician before the procedure.

5. **What's the hospital stay?**

   Laparoscopic surgery usually involves a one- or two-night stay. A traditional "open" prostatectomy can mean two or three nights, maybe longer, depending on how you heal.

6. **How long before you can lift things?**

   You won't be allowed to lift anything heavier than 10 lbs for the first six weeks of your recovery.

7. **When can I drive?**

   You'll be allowed to drive after the catheter comes out—usually in about a week, so long as you're off the narcotic pain meds.

8. **How about going back to work?**

   A good rule of thumb is three to four weeks. Some guys go back earlier, some later; it depends on how you feel and how your body is healing. Don't push it. You'll know when you're ready.

9. **How soon can I travel after surgery?**

   Some men travel with a catheter still in place, but it wouldn't be my recommendation. Your energy will be seriously depleted after surgery and getting through an airport is enough hassle when you feel *good*. Since you can't lift anything heavier than 10 lbs for the first six weeks anyway, I would suggest waiting at least until then.

### 10. How long will I have a catheter?

About one week on average.

### 11. How uncomfortable is the catheter?

Using the same one to ten pain scale, I would rank catheterization at about a two. It's more uncomfortable than painful. There's just something about having a tube sticking out of your penis that's a little unsettling at first. The good news is that you get used to it fairly quickly.

### 12. Does it hurt to have the catheter removed?

No. In fact, it's over so fast you won't even have time to consider it.

### 13. Will I be incontinent?

At first, just about everyone is incontinent. You just had a tube sticking out of your penis for the past week and it did all of the urinating for you. Now, you're back on your own. You have only one urinary sphincter (you had *two* before surgery) and you have to train your muscles to do double duty. It takes a little time—or a lot of time—depending on your recovery.

### 14. What can I do to protect myself from accidents?

There are several good incontinence products on the market. My personal favorite is Depends Guards for Men. They'll provide the protection you need for as long as you need it.

### 15. How about fathering children?

No. Once your prostate is removed, you will not be able to reproduce unless, of course, you had your sperm frozen before surgery.

### 16. Can I still ejaculate?

No. Your ability to ejaculate is removed along with your prostate. No prostate…no ejaculation. You will, however, be able to have an orgasm, even if you're unable to achieve an erection. It will be a "dry" orgasm and you may find it's even more intense than what you experienced before surgery.

### 17. Will I be impotent?

You won't be able to have an erection with the catheter in place. After it's removed, a lot depends on your age and the stage of the disease when you were diagnosed. If your surgeon was able to spare any of the nerve bundles that control erections (there are two sets—one set on each side of the prostate), your chances improve. These days, there's hope for virtually everyone thanks to advances in ED drugs, penile injections, penile suppositories, vacuum erection devices (VEDs), and penile implants. Consider them your friends and your sex life can be as fulfilling as ever, for you and your spouse.

### 18. Are penile injections painful?

Surprisingly, no. The needles are the same used for insulin injections and they're short, sharp, and hair thin. The most painful thing about penile injections is gathering the courage to try it—once. When you overcome that, it's really easy.

### 19. What are my chances for survival?

Good. If your cancer is caught in the earliest stage, the American Cancer Society places your chances of surviving five years or more at almost 100 percent.

### 20. Will my cancer come back?

It's possible, but if detected early, your chances are good that it won't return. Your physician will examine the pathology report and chart the best course of action for you.

**21. What's the follow-up?**

You'll have a PSA test every ninety days for the first year. If your PSA remains undetectable, you will be tested every six months the second year and then be checked annually for the rest of your life.

# Day 300

Where do we go from here?

Since I was diagnosed, I've struggled with this question. What does this watershed event mean to me? What does it mean for however much life I have left? What is God trying to tell me?

It's an enigma wrapped in a riddle. I honestly do not know.

The moment I think I might be on to an answer, I get more questions. The times I think there are nothing *but* questions, I get answers. It's tough, this cancer stuff. But I wonder if, in some small way, that maybe that's all there is to it. Questions. Answers. Watching. Waiting. It's enough to drive a sane man crazy and a crazy man to barricade himself in a cave.

Through it all, I have tried to maintain my faith, my courage, my hope and, most of all, my sense of humor. I've even written jokes about prostate cancer (OK, they're not very funny); I've tried to see this disease from every angle. It's like playing 3D Chinese checkers with your body as the game board. Every time you look at it, you see something different. Sometimes, the most obvious things aren't so obvious at all. Other times you get exactly what you see—nothing more.

I comfort myself in what I believe to be the "facts." I know my diagnosis. I've read the pathology report. I've researched the statistics on my "survivability," and I know my chances of regaining a "normal" sex life.

If this challenge was designed to throw me into the abyss and have me emerge through some spiritual journey, then I guess it's succeeded. Cancer has changed me spiritually. I pray regularly (sometimes incessantly), and I have seen my share of miracles.

What does all this mean?

I am beginning to think there are no real answers. I suspect that we get what we get and we're supposed to do our best with it. Search if you want and you may find something, but what you may find is that there is only more searching to be done.

For the time being, I have resolved just to "be." That doesn't mean I have to accept things the way they are. I, however, recognize that God—for whatever reason—has given me another opportunity to live my life. And while I linger in this limbo land between doctors and destiny, I am at least happy to be here.

No matter where I go next.

———

# EPILOGUE

## Day 365

One year later...

That's the way they used to tell a story in the old movies. You'd see something happen and then pages would fly off the calendar or the screen would just fade to black and the words *"One Year Later"* would appear on the screen. That's pretty much where I find myself today. One year later...

Here's where I stand.

## I am tired.

This year has been an emotional roller coaster.

This very moment, one year ago today, I was poring over the *Prostate Cancer for Dummies* book. It's true; there really is a "Dummies" book about prostate cancer. I skimmed it, searching for clues that might help me understand what I was fighting. I read it at such a fevered pace that I missed two-thirds of the information. I was just looking for immediate answers. Something this disease doesn't give you.

One thing I've learned is that the only thing immediate about cancer is that it can kill you quickly if you're unlucky enough to have the *wrong* kind. It can kill you slowly if you have the *right* kind. Basically, what you learn is that it's a killer that can be slowed down, even stopped, but you'll probably sleep with one eye open the rest of your life.

## I am impotent.

There's nothing else to say.

# I am fortunate.

I have a loving wife who tells me repeatedly that it does not matter. Charlotte has embraced the "new normal" with a spirit and vitality unmatched by mere mortals. In Charlotte's world, there is hope. There is ALWAYS hope.

*"It's early,"* she'll say to me as a means of comfort.

*"The doctors all say it's early. Give it time. You'll see,"* she'll add.

*"And if it turns out the other way?"* I'll ask, the perennial pessimist.

*"If it does, we'll deal with that then. The important thing is that we have time. That's something we thought we had lost. We got it back. Let's enjoy it,"* she'll add.

Of course I KNOW she's right. That's part of what makes this so damn hard. It is a lesson I have had to learn and relearn and then learn all over again. The hardest lesson to learn about this disease is that one thing that should be etched above the doorway of every urologist's office in the world: <u>It just takes time.</u>

# I am continent.

I learned this lesson firsthand in my battle for continence. Yes, I have become continent (something I thought I would never regain) and it only took six months. Half a year of going from a catheter to diapers, to pads to panty liners *(made for a woman, but strong enough for a man!)* and ultimately back to boxers. It was one *hell* of a lot of fun.

It is a peculiar thing, potty training at the ripe old age of forty-eight. It isn't much fun, but, as humiliating as this is/was, it is still better than being impotent. Don't get me wrong. I do not want to return to those days—ever. But, at least, I thought I could see progress here (on an almost glacial scale). Progress IS progress, however, and I was happy to be making some.

# I am cancer free.

This, of course, is the best deal of all. I know I am at least partially to blame for my impotence because I am the one, after all, that told Dr. Lee, *"When in doubt, cut it out."*

Knowing what I know today, I stand behind that statement. And if I had it do all over again, I would tell him the same thing. Cancer FREE is a good thing. No. It's a GREAT thing.

So this brings us to the end of our journey. In some ways, I will miss this journal. In other ways, I will not. It has been a companion when times were tough. It has been a confidant when I couldn't find the words to say aloud to myself or to the people who loved me. It has been my confessor and collaborator. It has gotten me through the most difficult time in my life. And it is that life, with all of its uncertainty, that I face each day with a scarlet C painted fire engine red on my damaged psyche.

What's next? I wish I knew. Then again, maybe I don't. All I can say right now is that I ran the race and crossed the finish line.

In the 1968 Summer Olympics, a Tanzanian marathon runner named John Akhwari got separated from the pack and became lost in the rabbit warren that is Mexico City. He fell down and cut himself. He was disoriented when he stumbled into the Olympic stadium an hour after every other runner had crossed the finish line.

When asked why he hadn't just given up, he said:

*"My country did not send me seven thousand miles to start the race. They sent me seven thousand miles to finish."*

———

*"Let's have a hand for that young cowboy and wish him better luck next time; And hope we see him up in Fargo or somewhere farther down the line. This time he sure drew a bad one, one that nobody could ride. But by the way he pulled his hat on, you knew he'd be there for the fight."*

"Farther Down the Line"
Written by Lyle Lovett

# RESOURCES

## *Prostate Cancer Web Resources*

New York Prostate Institute
www.nyprostate.org

Patient Advocates for Advanced Cancer Treatment
www.paactusa.org

The Hypertext Guide to Prostate Cancer
www.hypertext.org

United States Library of Medicine – National Institutes of Health
www.nlm.nih.gov

Us Too Prostate Cancer Education and Support
www.prostatepointers.org

WebMD
www.webmd.com/prostate-cancer/

You Are Not Alone Now Prostate Cancer Support Site
www.yananow.net/

## *General Prostate Cancer Resources*

*A Primer on Prostate Cancer: The Empowered Patient's Guide*
by Stephen B. Strum and Donna Pogliano

American Foundation for Urologic Disease
300 W. Pratt St., Suite 401
Baltimore, MD 21201-2463
(800) 828-7866
www.urologyhealth.org

American Prostate Society
P.O. Box 870
Hanover, MD 21076
(800) 308-1106
www.ameripros.org

Cleveland Clinic Health Information Center
www.clevelandclinic.org/health

National Institute on Aging
Age Page: Prostate Problems
Federal Building, Room 6C12 9000
Bethesda, MD 20892
(301) 496-1752

National Kidney and Urologic Diseases Information Clearinghouse
3 Information Way
Bethesda, MD 20892-3560
E-mail: nkudic@info.niddk.nih.gov

The Cleveland Clinic Foundation
Urological Institute
9500 Euclid Avenue
Cleveland, OH 44195
(216) 444-2200 or (800) 223-2273
www.clevelandclinic.org/urology

Tower Urology
Cedars-Sinai Medical Office Tower
8631 West 3rd Street 915E
Los Angeles, CA 90048
310-854-9898 or (888) 24-TOWER
www.towerurology.com/

Urology Associates of North Texas
811 West Interstate 20, Suite 114
Arlington TX 76017
(817) 784-8268
www.uant.com

Urology Channel
www.urologychannel.com

US Too International, Inc.
930 N. York Road, Suite 50
Hinsdale, IL 60521-2993
(800) 808-7866
www.ustoo.com

Zero The Project to End Prostate Cancer
10 G Street NE, Suite 601
Washington, DC 20002
(888) 245-9455
www.zerocancer.org

## *General Cancer Resources*

American Cancer Society
1599 Clifton Road, NE
Atlanta, GA 30329-4251

(800) 227-2345 or (404) 320 3333
www.cancer.org

Association of Oncology Social Work
4700 W. Lake Ave.
Glenview, IL 60025-1485
(847) 375-4721
E-mail: info@cancer411.org
www.cancer411.org

CancerAnswers
5575 Baltimore Drive, Suite 105-221
La Mesa, CA 91942
(888) 226-8287
Fax: (619) 287-6528
Email: DrStillwell@CancerAnswers.com
www.canceranswers.com

Cancer Care Inc.
275 7th Ave.
New York, NY 10001
(212) 302-2400 or (800) 813-HOPE (4673)
Email: feedback@cancerpage.com
www.cancerpage.com/

National Cancer Institute
31 Center Dr., MSC 2580
Bethesda, MD 20892-2580

CancerNet: http://cancernet.nci.nih.gov

Cancer Clinical Trials

http://cancertrials.nci.nih.gov
NCI Public Inquiries Office
Building 31
Room 10A03, 31 Center Drive
MSC 2580
Bethesda, MD 20892-2580
(301) 435-3848

OncoLink
A University of Pennsylvania Cancer Center Resource
www.oncolink.upenn.edu/

Oncology.com
www.oncology.com

The Cancer Information Service
(800) 422-6237 ((800) 4-CANCER)

## ABOUT THE AUTHOR

Robert "Bob" Hill, fifty-four, is a prostate cancer survivor who lives in Colleyville, Texas, with his wife Charlotte. They have one son, Cole Garner Hill, who is a music journalist. Bob and Charlotte own a public relations firm and produce The Boomer Brief, www.boomerbrief.com, a Web site dedicated to keeping baby boomers current on the world around them.

7117984R0

Made in the USA
Charleston, SC
23 January 2011